Violence In

THE REALITY BEHIND VIOLENT CRIME

Elie Godsi

Constable · London

First published in Great Britain 1999
by Constable and Company Limited,
3 The Lanchesters,
162 Fulham Palace Road,
London W6 9ER
Copyright © Elie Godsi 1999
ISBN 0 09 478140 0
The right of Elie Godsi to be identified as author of this work
has been asserted by him in accordance with
the Copyright, Designs and Patents Act 1988

Set in Linotron Sabon 10.5pt by
Rowland Phototypesetting Limited
Printed in Great Britain by
St Edmundsbury Press Ltd,
both of Bury St Edmunds, Suffolk

A CIP catalogue record for this book
is available from the British Library

For Richard Marshall

Contents

Acknowledgements

There are inevitably many people who have in one way or another helped to influence and shape the ideas in this book and wherever possible I have acknowledged the contribution they have made either in the text or in the footnotes. There are others to whom I am indebted for their support at work. There are too many to mention and too many to thank individually, but among them are the colleagues with whom I have worked over recent years at Beaconfield, especially Sue, Deb, Colin, Bev, Heidi and Carol; I am very appreciative of their support through difficult times. Thanks also to Lesley Curtis for her professionalism and her sense of humour, to Pat Weston for her enthusiasm and kindness at work, and to Lorna Bushnell for her acceptance and for being a great boss to work for. I would also like to thank David Dean for coming to my rescue when my monitor blew up during a crucial phase of writing. I would also like to express my gratitude to Carol O'Brien for her endless patience while awaiting the arrival of the manuscript and for the continual deadline extensions. I would particularly like to thank David Smail. His support and encouragement have been invaluable, and his gift with the written word has been an inspiration to me as well as to so many others. He has dared to speak compassionately on behalf of people in distress; to set aside received wisdom and professional mythology and, above all else, to understand that distress is not the fault of those experiencing it. He deserves all the peace he can find in a superficial world.

I also have to thank the many people I have worked with clinically over the years. Each of them in their own way has dared to speak the truth and taken great personal risks in telling me what has happened to them or what they themselves have done. They have all contributed to this book and have helped to further my own understanding of the difficult and painful realities that I have written about. I sincerely hope that I have done justice to their experiences.

More than anyone else I have my wife to thank, for without her this book would literally not have been written. Her support, her limitless patience and her encouragement in the many, many months of writing have all been invaluable. She has made a thousand sacrifices to enable me to write and has put up with me over a long period of creative tension; more than this, she has also given up countless hours of her time to read through and skilfully edit the various draft versions of each of the chapters. She has added immeasurably to the final shape the words have taken.

Introduction

One of the reasons I was attracted to the possibility of writing this book was that it was intended to be read by anyone who has an interest in the subject of violence, not just by a professional or academic audience. For this reason, I have had relative freedom to write in a manner that does not adhere to the rather limited ways that the academic or scientific communities impose, and the rigid use of language that they define as legitimate.

I have based much of what is in these pages on my experience of working with people who have been violent, and many who have been the victims of violence. Personal clinical and professional experience is as valid a source of 'evidence' as any other, but that experience also needs to be informed and guided by other forms of knowledge and other sources of valid information. Conversely, professional or academic knowledge in the form of research findings or statistical information can easily become meaningless and unhelpful without being subject to the important component of personal experience and judgement. Both should complement one another, and wherever it has been appropriate I have used as many different forms of 'evidence' as possible to back up any assertions that I have made. In many cases, I have used the Notes section at the end of the book to give the reader further information, or to expand or clarify a specific point made in the main body of text.

The central aim of this book is to try to explain why people behave violently. It is not my intention to excuse or condone violence in any way; attempting to understand why something happens is certainly not the same as condoning it or accepting it. However, once we gain a fuller understanding of other people, especially those whose actions are defined as being beyond explanation, then we stand a greater chance of being able to discard whatever prejudices and misconceptions we have about them. Only then can we begin to view them with the degree of humanity they deserve. In any case, how any given society at any period in its history defines 'otherness', or those whom it defines as 'evil' or 'mad', always reveals more about that society and its values than about those who are defined as 'abnormal'. Making sense of violence and examining the misconceptions we have about it therefore also involves examining how we view our own humanity.

Understanding why people behave violently is both a very complex matter and a very simple one. There are many levels of explanation and many reasons why people express themselves in brutal ways, but that complexity should not be used to conceal simple truths. As we are living in an age in which the importance of individualistic explanations are heavily emphasised and exaggerated, those truths are easily and readily obscured. Because we don't have a collective framework to make sense of violence without referring to personal responsibility and individual choice, it is all too easy to resort to moral condemnation and to apportion blame. Responsibility is much too important a moral imperative to be reduced to the level of individuals. Families, communities, companies, governments and entire societies can behave irresponsibly, yet it is very much harder to apportion blame when they do. As we approach the end of the twentieth century, all manner of professional explanations for violence tend to focus on the individual and grossly to exaggerate the contribution of biological, genetic and psychological factors as opposed to environmental ones. As with a moral framework of individual responsibilities, the obsession with which individual factors are elaborated upon and pursued, which has come to dominate how we view and explain violence, is not only misleading, but is in many cases misguided. It is a travesty that the only ideological framework that affords even the possibility of avoiding notions of blame is a medical one which ultimately explains violence in terms of faulty biology and genetics. This book is an attempt to counter the imbalanced emphasis on individuals and to offer an essentially environmental explanation for violence. To do this not only means trying to explain the personal experiences that shape individual people's behaviour, but also requires a field of view that extends far beyond the individual. We are all shaped and influenced by the conditions we find ourselves in, and the experiences we have over the course of our lives, to a much greater degree than is commonly accepted.

It is important to emphasize that this is not a book about 'treatment'; though I am critical of the way in which many people are dealt with throughout the mental health services, and particularly in relation to psychiatry, I am not specifically concerned here with what to do with people once they have become violent. My aim is to suggest ways in which we might view the problem of violence that might offer a possibility of prevention. My criticisms about those professions who are charged with dealing with violent offenders are not centrally about their attempts to 'treat' those people they work with, except in as much as their methods of treatment systematically obscure the realities behind the violence or the distress they are routinely presented with. The central problem is that the imperative to control such people, the methods of treatment available (usually some form of chemical sedation or another), and the pragmatic need to do something quickly about their behaviour or experience all give rise to hopeless confusion between cause and explanation. The fact that a violent individual perceives the world in a particular way that is unhelpful, or are knocked out by a particular drug, says very little about why they are violent in the first place: yet all too often these methods of 'treatment' and social control are completely inverted, presented as original cause, and offered as explanation.

In as much as this book is about those who express themselves violently, it is also concerned with those who are victims of violence and the consequences of being victimized: the two are closely linked. I therefore need to emphasize that while I am drawing strong links between the experience of personal distress ('mental health problems') and violence, I am certainly not suggesting that all people who are 'distressed' are going to be violent. Those who are experiencing personal distress have a hard enough time being stigmatized and misunderstood as it is.

With the exception of certain high-profile cases that have received extensive amounts of (extremely one-dimensional) media coverage, all of the stories or accounts of child abuse and violence in Chapter 1 are based on the real experiences of many people I have known and worked with. Their identities have obviously been concealed and altered, although this in no way diminishes the accuracy of their experiences. I have attempted to do justice to the accounts of violence by writing accurately about them. This has not been done in any way to dramatize or sensationalize the accounts or to exaggerate their impact. It is all too easy these days to glibly refer to, say, 'sexual' abuse, yet leave it as an abstract idea with little or no significance attached to it. Academic and professional uses of language, particularly in the more learned scientific papers and journals, insist on a detached and supposedly 'objective' style of writing that promotes an impersonal pomposity that such issues do not deserve.

The brief scenarios in Chapter 1 are truthful and unexaggerated accounts of the kinds of brutality and cruelty that I hear on a regular, almost daily basis in the clinical and therapeutic NHS setting in which I have worked over the last decade: accounts told me by so many of the people I have worked with, often with a great deal of trepidation and distress, in their attempts to make sense of their confusing experience of a brutal world. I am indebted to them for their courage in daring to speak out. Their experiences deserve to be heard outside of the closeted setting of the therapy room. If these accounts are disturbing to read, then they should be; violence and child abuse are disturbing matters and we should be moved by such experiences. I have presented these scenarios in Chapter 1 at face value without any attempt at explanation.

Compassion is something that has become hard to find in a

world in which we are forced, or at least encouraged, to compete with one another for meagre resources, to blame each other when life is hard, and to view each other and our relationships as marketable commodities. Nowhere is this lack of compassion more evident than for those who behave violently, and especially those high-profile cases in which children are harmed. Violent offenders are often the focus of extreme vilification and they are all too readily 'demonized' and stripped of their humanity. More than this, they have become the focus for everything that seems to have gone wrong in public life and they are scapegoated and blamed for all of society's ills. It does indeed seem hard to be compassionate to those who, through their own actions, deny others their humanity or even their lives. Yet such people are no less deserving of our humanity than anyone else, and in many cases all the more so for what they themselves have experienced. It is my sincerest wish that this book may contribute in some way to a climate in which all victims of violence can speak freely about their experiences and that they are listened to with compassion and, above all else, that they are believed – whoever they are, and whatever they themselves may have done.

·1·

Perpetrators and Victims

Derek

It was a very ordinary afternoon on a sunny June day. There were only a few people drinking in the Curton Arms pub, and the two men who had seen each other before on previous afternoons exchanged greetings. Despite the obvious difference in age between them and the fact that they were relative strangers, they seemed to have enough in common to pass the afternoon in each other's company. One of them was in his early twenties and other was a young-looking man in his fifties. The younger man was softly spoken and evidently quite shy. In fact, he had few friends and was glad for the company and the interest that the older man was showing in him. Over the course of the afternoon they drank several pints of beer and chatted about football: who was playing well at the time, and what they thought about the England team. At closing time, the younger man invited his companion back to the home that he shared with his mother. He had proudly told him that he had bought a bottle of whisky the night before and that there was plenty left of it for them both to drink. This way, they could continue their drinking and football talk, which in fact they did for the remainder of the afternoon. By early evening, they had finished the bottle of whisky.

The two men then began to argue, but although voices were

raised, the younger man's mother (who was resting upstairs) thought little of what was going on. But then the shouting got louder and she heard a man cry out, as if in horrific pain; in an instant, though, the silence returned. She quickly got out of bed and went downstairs, only to find her son with a kitchen knife in his hand, standing over the collapsed body of the older man. There was blood all over the man on the floor and also her son's hands. The young man stood there motionless, almost as if frozen, barely acknowledging that his mother was there, seemingly staring right through her. She screamed and ran out of the house, not knowing where she was going or what to do. All she knew was that she had to run away, though her reaction was one of confusion and blind panic rather than fear for her own safety. She ran to a neighbour's house and knocked frantically on the door. When the neighbour answered, all she could do was ask them to call an ambulance. She found that she could barely speak as she felt unable to breathe, and the shocking images of the scene she had just witnessed kept flashing through her mind, her son's expressionless face staring right through her. All she could do was keep repeating that there had been a terrible accident.

When the ambulance arrived a short time later, the older man was still alive but unconscious. He was losing blood and had heavy internal bleeding as the single knife wound had pierced his left lung. He was lucky, the blade had missed his heart by a matter of millimetres. Another centimetre to the left and he would almost certainly have been dead by the time the ambulance arrived. Such is the fine line between life and death. When the police appeared a short time later, the younger man was still in the same room where the attack had happened. He was sitting silently on a sofa next to the bloody carpet, and said nothing when he was arrested or for several hours after. He could not explain what had happened, nor why he had reacted in the way he had.

Though she tried desperately to make sense of what had happened, his mother was equally shocked and confused. She was also acutely ashamed, wondering what the neighbours would think and knowing that it would all be reported in the local paper. She wondered what she had done wrong as a mother and whether she would be blamed for her son's actions. She knew that her life had been a hard one and that she had struggled to cope. She had many regrets about some of the things she had done as a mother, and now all of these came back to haunt her. If things had been different, perhaps this might not have happened. What would the victim's family think of her?

She could not understand it. Though he would lose his temper from time to time, for the most part her son was mild-mannered and easy-going, to the extent that he would rarely argue or disagree with anybody. In fact, she had often told him off for being a 'soft touch' because he was easily led and taken advantage of. He had never been this violent before, so why he had attacked this comparative stranger was a complete mystery.

A short while later in the police cell, she asked her son to explain his actions. He simply apologized to her repeatedly, saying that he had drunk too much and lost his temper. That was all, there was nothing more to it. After that, there was an unspoken agreement between them that they would never again mention or speak about what had happened.

During the course of the police investigations they found the young man to be very quietly spoken and barely articulate. He spoke little, and what he did say did not always make complete sense to them. Then it was discovered that he had been sent to a 'special school' as a child, and had therefore been classed as educationally 'sub-normal', of 'low intelligence'. Eventually he was convicted of Actual Bodily Harm, wounding with intent, and sentenced to be detained in a secure hospital under the Mental Health Act due to his 'mental impairment'. The mystery of his unprecedented act of violence was solved with reference to his limited intellect, and the fact that he had been drinking heavily on the day of the attack.

His victim largely recovered from his physical wounds, though even several years later he still felt occasional pain and discomfort. The psychological and emotional trauma of his experience continued to bother him in the form of 'flashbacks' and unwanted recollections of the attack. He always felt anxious being around anyone with knives, even if it was just sitting around a table having a meal.

Robert and Jon

On 12 February 1993, two-year-old James Bulger went missing while out with his mother in Bootle's Strand shopping centre in Liverpool. The British nation watched in disbelief and horror at the hazy images from a security video which showed tiny James being led away by the hand by the two boys who were to become his killers. These haunting images of tragedy were broadcast around the world as a moment of betrayal was captured on film for ever. A total of twenty-six witnesses came forward to say that they had seen two older boys with a crying toddler over the course of the 2½-mile journey to the railway track where James's brutalized body was later discovered. The police were shocked when they realized how small, and therefore how young, the abductors were. Just two days after James's disappearance they arrested two unnamed ten-year-old boys. Since the killers were such young children, the moral ramifications of this death profoundly affected the country, and the case became a focus for widespread unease about the state of the nation. Amid the shock and disbelief, there were countless explanations put forward; everyone was talking about it, everyone had their opinions and explanations.

On 24 November 1993, at the end of their trial at Preston Crown Court, Jon Venables and Robert Thompson, both aged eleven, became the youngest convicted murderers in Britain for almost 250 years. Britain is the only country in Western Europe that allows ten-year-olds to be held criminally responsible and, if they kill, to be tried by judge and jury as if they are adults. Despite the improvements in juvenile courts and the provision of video links, the boys were subjected to a full trial in front of the all-consuming media eye. At the end of eight months' investigation by 120 police officers, a seventeen-day trial involving some of the most distinguished and eminent members of the legal and psychiatric professions, the reasons for these two boys to have behaved so cruelly and brutally were never even touched upon. The sole purpose of the trial was to prove whether Jon Venables and Robert Thompson had killed James Bulger or not, and whether they knew that what they were doing to James was wrong. No explanation, however complex or difficult, was ever explored. At the end of the entire judicial process no one was any the wiser in terms of answering the one question that everyone who had heard about the case was grappling with: why?

Doris

Police were alerted to the scene at the small council house by a neighbour who reported that there had been a murder. They were unprepared for what they saw. A woman in her early twenties had killed her four-year-old son and her grandfather. The bodies were found in bed in different rooms, each had been suffocated. The woman herself was found looking dishevelled and agitated, she kept repeating herself over and over, muttering about meningitis and how she had tried to help. Over and over, she said Jesus was involved; Jesus was a compassionate man; Jesus would not allow them to suffer any more. The police could not make sense of what she was saying, and she was arrested and immediately assessed by the police psychiatrist. As she was clearly delusional and incoherent, he pronounced her to be suffering from a psychotic illness. Her incoherent statements about Jesus were quite classic delusions: a clear case of schizophrenia.

There was quite a scandal in the local papers when the story became public, especially when it was revealed that the woman had only recently been released from a local psychiatric hospital. She was known to local mental health services and had spent short periods of time as an in-patient for her schizophrenia. Why had the doctors released her? Surely they must have known she was mad? Another scandal, another case of a schizophrenic killer unleashed on to an unsuspecting community. The chief executive of the local NHS Trust spoke directly to the local media and insisted that there was no way any of those who had been treating her could have foreseen or predicted what she would later do. She had seemed unusually well and cheerful when they had last assessed her in hospital, and was deemed fit enough to return home for a long weekend. It was true that no one had been to see her at home after she had been discharged into the community, but this was not unusual given that she was due to return to the hospital only a short while after the day of the killings. Despite the protests from the remaining relatives of the family involved, no one was to blame: the psychiatrists who had been treating her for several years could not have predicted what was to happen.

Yet still many questions remained unanswered for the local community and the relatives of the woman and her victims. How could a mother kill her own son? How could she kill her own grandfather? Few people actually knew her, and those who did were shocked and stunned. She had been going to the local church, but her attendance had been irregular. They knew her to be a friendly and mild-mannered woman who generally kept herself to herself, but was always eager to please and be helpful.

She was eventually assessed as unfit to plead. As she was clearly 'mentally ill' she was convicted of the manslaughter of her grandfather and her son. Under the Mental Health Act, she was ordered to be detained for an indefinite period at a maximum secure 'special' hospital. Since she was evidently psychotic, she would not be released until her illness was properly treated or at least brought under sustained control. Under the terms of her detention she would require the approval of the Home Secretary before she could ever be considered for release. This would need to be for at least a period of several years, before she could be considered safe enough to be gradually released back into the community.

Fred and Rose

Towards the end of February 1994, police began to show an interest in the family living at 25 Cromwell Street in Gloucester. Suspicions were growing about the parents of the household, Fred and Rose West, whose daughter Heather had last been seen in 1987 when she was sixteen. Her parents first claimed that she had left home in a blue mini with a lesbian friend, then Rose had told police she had given her £600 to help her on her way and that Heather had phoned them. Their accounts of her disappearance, as well as other events, were beginning to reveal many anomalies and thus the investigation intensified.

Fred West, a builder by trade, was known as a hard worker but also as a somewhat 'odd' man by his work colleagues. He would at times tell of horrific accidents that he had seen on his way to work, giving vivid descriptions of the bodies and injuries at these fictitious scenes. Over the years that he had lived in Cromwell Street, Fred had carried out many renovations and extensions to his house. The upper floors had been divided into small single bedsits that had for many years been let to students or to other temporary lodgers. The first floor had been converted into a bar with a bedroom next to it. Another bedroom on the top floor had a four-poster bed in it as well as hidden microphones and spotlights.

Some people living in the area were aware that Fred's wife Rose was a prostitute who worked from their home and who advertised her services as 'Mandy Mouse'. She had a regular flow of male and female customers coming to the house at Cromwell Street, and there was little attempt made to conceal this. She was even known to offer sex in return for favours such as repairing Fred's van. Others in the locality believed that the couple had what seemed to be an 'open' relationship, sleeping with whomever they pleased and enjoying sex parties with their friends. Though Fred was known to be a very possessive and jealous man, he encouraged his wife in her profession and enjoyed watching her having sex with other men and women.

When police investigations began, no one knew the horrific nature – nor the extent – of the crimes that would be discovered. Excavations on the house revealed a total of nine bodies buried underneath the house and patio, the first of which was Heather, their missing daughter. The other bodies all turned out to be young women, seven of whom had been 'in care' and were last seen alive at bus stops in the area, some as long ago as the 1970s. Another body was found in a different house that had previously been occupied by Fred, and was that of Fred's daughter Charmaine by his first marriage, who had disappeared in 1971. Two more bodies were found buried in a field close to where Fred had grown up in the village of Much Marcle near the Forest of Dean. As police had suspected, one of these last two bodies proved to be Fred's first wife, 'Rena' Costello, the mother of Charmaine who had disappeared in 1968.

Fred was arrested and charged with murder as soon as the excavations began to reveal the contents of the 'house of horror' at Cromwell Street. Rose was not arrested immediately, but she was subsequently charged with the murder of their daughter Heather, as well as with other offences including rape and assisted rape.

As the trial unfolded the public heard of systematic child abuse and prostitution, perversion, sexual torture and terrible acts of brutality and violence spanning over thirty years. Fred had microphones in every room, and pornographic videotapes were frequently being played, some of which Fred had taken of family members. Both Fred and Rose were routinely physically and sexually violent towards their children. With Rose's help, he 'initiated' Anne-Marie when she was eight years old in the basement room at Cromwell Street. Rose was said to have held the children by the throat and to have smiled and laughed while they were being sexually abused. Anne-Marie was even told by her parents that she would one day be grateful for what they had done. Frequently beaten by Rose, Anne-Marie learned to hide the injuries and survived by becoming passive and acquiescent. She was later sexually abused by her grandfather, Rose's father. As a teenager she was regularly sexually abused by her father, often in his work van. From the age of thirteen she was made to sleep with Rose's clients, for which she was sometimes given a box of chocolates. At the age of fifteen, she ran away from Cromwell Street and lived on the streets; at times she would agree to sex with strangers just for a roof over her head. Despite having been a victim, during the trial itself Anne-Marie had bricks thrown through her windows and was taunted by locals. In the midst of her evidence she was taken to hospital after taking an overdose of alcohol and prescribed drugs.

The evidence heard about the manner of the killings was as terrible as the accounts from those who had escaped death. The remains of Shirley Hubbard showed that she had been bound with adhesive tape up to eye level and a plastic tube had been inserted into her nostril. She had been kept alive in this way, just able to breathe but unable to make a sound while she was subjected to days of sexual torture. Many of the other victims had been bound with tape or belts as well. Some had been battered so hard with a hammer-like object that their skulls were fractured. Shirley Robinson had been pregnant when she was killed. More than forty people, among them relatives, friends and police officers, have received counselling from Victim Support in Gloucester in connection with the case: the jury were also offered this form of support, as were the journalists covering the case.

Journalists and crime writers queued to acquire contracts to write about the story, but had to wait for the trial to be heard some many months later before they could profit from doing so. Fred is believed to have fired one solicitor acting on his behalf because he had negotiated to sell his story of his involvement in the case. Fred himself is said to have been writing his autobiography while he was detained in prison awaiting the trial.

Fred West's last ever act was also to be a violent one. He hung himself in his prison cell on New Year's Day, in 1995. He left a note for his wife Rose, and at the same time left her to face the process of justice on her own. Rose was already in some distress. In 1992 she took an overdose of tablets and alcohol and her stomach was pumped out in Gloucester Royal hospital. She was also treated for depression. In prison she took to eating and put on over 3 stone in weight. On 21 and 22 November 1995, Rose was convicted of the ten murders of young women and girls. Police announced that they were trying to trace the whereabouts of at least nine other young women who were missing, and who had had known contacts with Fred and Rose.

Albert

An elderly man in his early sixties develops what he sees as a loving relationship with his own granddaughter. She is only eight years old, but he knows that she is not treated well by her parents who seem to have little or no time for her. Indeed, he seems to sense instinctively that she is a lonely and very needy child. At first he gains her trust by playing with her and giving her sweets. He starts by sitting her on his knee and pretending that she is on a train that is chugging along the line. Starved of both affection and attention, she is naturally drawn to him because he is the only person who shows any interest in her; the only attention she gets from her parents is when she is being told off or punished. Most of the time her father is not there and her mother shows little or no interest in her. Her 'granddaddy' seems so different, he seems fun to be with. Everyone notices how she loves her granddad, how 'special' their public relationship is.

When they are on their own, however, he is quite different. He then starts to get her to do things that confuse her and that she is unsure about. He checks inside her pants to 'see how she is growing', and then tells her to play with his penis. He makes her jump up and down on his lap and then he hurts her, he squeezes her too hard; she protests by making a sound, but he ignores her. She dare not say anything because she has learnt from her parents that she must do as she is told at all times, otherwise she will be punished. When he has finished squeezing her, he is loving again, tells her that she is such a good girl (he is the only one who ever praises her), and then gives her a bar of chocolate.

Granddad often stays in the house now because his wife, the girl's grandmother, died some years before and he is a lonely man who only has his family left. Everyone feels sorry for him because he seems so frail and is on his own much of the time; besides which, he seems to derive so much pleasure from being with his grandchildren. It is at night, however, when everyone has gone to sleep that he is at his most vicious. It is at night that he comes to his granddaughter's bedroom and wakes her up. It is at night that he lifts her nightie and anally abuses her, forcing her face into the pillow so that she does not make a sound and so that she can barely breathe. He need not worry, for though she feels as if she is being stabbed from behind and in spite of the terrible pain, she dare not make any noise; hers

PERPETRATORS AND VICTIMS

is a silent scream that no one will ever hear. Though she knows
that something is wrong, that this should not be happening, she
believes she will get into terrible trouble if anyone finds out. She
knows it must be her granddad doing this to her because she
recognizes his smell, but at the same time she is unsure if it *is*
him. Unlike at other times, this man says nothing to her. It is
somehow easier to believe that it is a 'monster' that comes into
her room at night, that this is not the same old man with whom
she has a 'special' relationship.

Each night this happens she is unable to sleep much because
of the terrible pain and sickness she feels in her stomach. The
pain is unbearable; it leaves her doubled up in agony. Unable
to control her brutalized bowels she wakes each morning to find
that she has soiled her sheets and her nightie. Every time this
happens she gets punished by her parents for being a bad girl
and for making her mother's life unnecessarily difficult. Her
father smacks her and then shoves her face into the shit to teach
her a lesson and to get her to stop doing it. As he holds her by
the neck he shouts into her face. She is never to do this again,
his voice rising to a crescendo as he finishes his sentence with
a scowling 'Do you understand?' She has learnt always to say
'yes' to him at this point through her tears. Her mother also
shouts at her and tells her she is a bad girl. All of this reinforces
the view that the child already has of herself as being bad. This
is the only way she can understand why she is being stabbed at
night in this way, because she must be very, very bad to deserve
to be hurt like this.

On one occasion some two years after the abuse started happening, she was talking to her mother about her grandfather.
She decided tentatively to mention that she believed that he
came in to her bedroom at night and that was why she continued
to be dirty and soiled in the morning. Her mother was furious
with her and slapped her across the face several times. Now she
really was in trouble, now she really was a bad girl for telling
such lies. Her mother did not mention what she had said to her
father or to her grandfather. Instead, she told them that she had
been lying and that God would punish her for being such a
wicked child.

27

So at the age of nine the girl was taken to church and spoken to by the local vicar who was also told that she was a wicked child who had been lying to her mother. She was terrified. The vicar spoke to her sternly, raising his voice and telling her of the punishment she would receive if she lied. God did not like children who lied. Jesus only loved good children who spoke the truth, did as they were told, and respected their parents. The vicar would pray for her, and she too would have to pray for forgiveness.

Margaret

This child is only five years old. She is frequently shouted at by her mother, Margaret, who stands over her and screams whenever she believes her daughter has done wrong. On other days, her mother beats her with a hairbrush or, the method she favours most, with a wooden cooking spoon. She often makes her daughter wait first before beating her, warning her that 'once we get home, then we'll see how clever you are', or 'just wait until I tell your father how bad you've been, wait until he gets home'. Margaret goes to church every Sunday and, as a religious woman, she believes that all children are born evil. She believes, therefore, that her daughter must not have a will of her own, that any hint of her own personality is a sign of trouble, a sign that she will become out of control.

She wants to control her daughter, her every move, her every thought. This is the only way to make sure she does not turn out to be a bad person. Her daughter can do little that is right in her mother's eyes. The beatings that Margaret inflicts on her daughter have little to do with the girl's behaviour and everything to do with her mother's moods at any given moment. Genuine mistakes or accidents are treated as deliberate signs of malice that need to be stamped out, as are any forms of childish behaviour or immaturity. The little girl is too young to understand this and so tries ever harder to please her mother; tries desperately to be good and to avoid making mistakes. The rules of this deadly game are unclear, for they are ever changing. One day she is being punished for something that usually passes unnoticed, but another day passes without incident when she is sure she will be attacked. She never really understands what it is she is supposed to have done, so that she quickly learns to always reply 'yes' when her mother accuses her of having done something. On the one occasion she said 'no', she learnt never to do so again.

From time to time, this young girl has to face the full might of her mother's viciousness: over and over, Margaret beats her daughter, over and over across her legs, her thighs, her bottom, only stopping when she becomes weary. If the girl cries out at any stage she will make it worse; any sign of tears or feelings will spur her mother on, and will merely prolong the beatings. There are days when the young girl tries to hide, especially after she has been warned, those terrible days when she knows that sooner or later the punishment will be meted out although she does not know when. She tries hiding under her bed, but when her mother finds her she is ridiculed, laughed at, and everyone is told how bad and naughty she is. Wherever her mother goes she tells people how naughty her daughter is: that she wets her bed; that she is dirty and bad for making such a mess. Sometimes Margaret washes her daughter after this, scrubbing her harshly and hurting her between her legs, telling her over and over how 'disgusting' and 'dirty' she is.

The young girl's father is away at work for much of the day and tries not to get involved in what is going on at home. He always sides with his wife and agrees with whatever she says, but is not directly involved in the beatings. He remains a bystander, a passive witness to the maltreatment of his daughter, preferring instead to avoid any conflict and have a 'quiet life'. In more private moments, on the very few occasions that his wife is not maintaining her vigil over her daughter's behaviour, he is actually quite kind and playful towards their child. His wife, however, resents any show of affection between them and does all she can to undermine any relationship they have. In private and in secret, she tells her daughter that if she misbehaves she will tell her father, who will take her to the market and give her away to the gypsies. Being only five years old, she believes her mother and is never quite able to trust her father again; she always remains on her guard in case this is the time that he will take her away. However bad her immature mind views life to be with her mother now, and however poorly formed her notions of running away are, nothing can ever be as bad as what the gypsies will do to her.

Betty

Betty had a baby daughter at the age of seventeen and called her Mary. Mary's father was not with Betty by the time she was born, and she grew up with another man whom Betty married when Mary was just ten months old. When Mary was born and placed into Betty's arms she jerked back and cried out, 'Take the "thing" away from me.' Even after some time had elapsed, Betty never appeared to have any joy or to derive pleasure from her daughter despite the adoration of her family over the 'bonny' baby. When Mary was one, she was discovered having swallowed a bottle of pills that her grandmother kept for her 'nerves'. She was rushed to hospital, her stomach was pumped, and little Mary recovered in time. No one asked at the hospital how a one-year-old baby had managed to climb on top of an old chest, open a drawer, reach to the back of the drawer to get the bottle of pills out from its hiding place, and then unscrew the top before swallowing enough of the bitter-tasting contents to almost kill herself. On several other occasions before she was five, there were further 'accidents' that had seriously threatened Mary's life. When Mary was three and a half she almost fell out of a third-floor open window while Betty was holding her over a sink, saved only by the quick reactions of an uncle who was in the room. Twice more over these early years, Mary had somehow managed to swallow tablets; and when she had her stomach pumped in hospital for the last time at the age of four, she repeatedly told staff that her mother had given her the 'smarties'. Betty told them not to believe her, that she was lying. After such a large number of 'accidents', relatives were growing increasingly suspicious that Betty had been trying to kill her own daughter. However, after this last incident with the tablets, Betty fell out with her family and disconnected herself from them.

Over the first five years of Mary's life, Betty repeatedly and regularly gave her away. On several occasions she left her and her younger brother with friends and relatives, stating she was unable to cope, only to return some time later to reclaim her children once more. On one occasion she handed her three-year-old daughter to a complete stranger at an adoption agency and walked out. At other times, Betty would leave her children with her husband and disappear for days on end. On her return, she and her husband would row and fight. Relatives and friends had repeatedly offered to adopt little Mary, for over all the periods of time that she was in their care they had grown fond of her, despite the increasingly obvious nature of her psychological disturbance: by the age of two she recoiled from physical affection; she was distant, detached and somehow unreachable. They said she never cried when hurt, she had temper tantrums, and stamped on the floor; and on one occasion when she was told her parents were coming to pick her up, she shouted at her uncle and hit him on the face with a toy gun that she had been playing with. Despite the offers to look after her and the growing concern of relatives, Mary remained with Betty. If she had been looked after elsewhere, her life would almost certainly have turned out differently. Such are the twists of fate upon which the direction of a life depends.

After Betty's decision to disconnect from her mother and sisters, there was no one to keep an effective eye on Mary. However, teachers documented her seemingly bizarre behaviour from the age of five, recalling how she would hide under her desk and lie there stiff as a rod. How she was frequently 'naughty' or else quiet and very withdrawn. She was said to be a very lonely child and unpopular with the other children whom she would be aggressive towards, often kicking, pinching or hitting them. Despite all the signs of behavioural and emotional disturbance that she displayed and the fact that she was constantly drawing attention to herself in one way or another, even if that involved punishment, no one had any idea at that time exactly what she was trying to draw their attention to. As is so often the case, some of her teachers deliberately chose to ignore her behaviour for fear of encouraging her: they thought little of what might be happening at home – after all, this was the 1950s and therefore not the era for alerting Child Guidance or Social Services. The more Mary drew attention to herself and her plight, the less it seemed to matter, and the worse and more aggressive her behaviour became. Still no one understood her cries for help. Indeed, her teachers commented that publicly Betty was fiercely protective of her children when she came to pick them up from school. Behind the reasonably well-turned-out public appearance of her children, though, there lay a private reality far more sinister than anyone concerned about Mary at that time was able to imagine, let alone believe.

Even before Mary started school at the age of five, she had already been forced to become involved in her mother's prostitution. At first, her mother would make her watch her having sex with her clients and then gradually she let her clients abuse Mary as well. At times Betty would hold Mary down, pulling her head back by her hair and pulling her arms behind her back while the men performed oral sex on her. At other times Mary was gagged and held down on her stomach. Years later all she could remember was the excruciating pain, perhaps they had anally abused her, the details were unclear because she was so confused about what had happened to her tiny body, but the pain was as vivid as if it had happened yesterday. All the time this was happening Betty held her down and gently reassured her that it wouldn't hurt for long. These men then stuck sharp objects into her legs and body, sticking them into her flesh and twisting them round. Many years later her adult body would remain scarred by these objects. After the men left, Betty would give Mary sweets and was gentle and loving towards her, laughing and playing games with her. This enforced child prostitution and sexual abuse occurred repeatedly over many years.

As Mary grew older, Betty became more and more dependent on alcohol and pills, and her mental and physical health deteriorated markedly with several stays in hospital. She also became increasingly cruel and verbally abusive towards her daughter. When Mary was six they moved into one of the worst streets of the worst slum in the area. It was a violent, rundown area of rat-infested houses, empty and derelict buildings, used car lots, warehouses and graffiti. Soon after the move Mary was attacked by a fourteen-year-old boy who stabbed her in the back with a broken bottle, leaving shards of glass in her that needed to be removed and the wound stitched. Their tiny home became filthy and Betty's husband would move in to look after the children when she was gone and then move out again when she returned. While Betty was at home her 'customers' visited her; at times they abused Mary as well and then left again.

Peter

Peter is a forty-one-year-old, highly successful sales and marketing director of a large insurance company. He has always prided himself on his commitment to his work and he has always worked long hours. As much as eighteen or twenty hours a day if required, and he is on call twenty-four hours, seven days a week. His work requires him to drive several hundred miles in a day all around the country, so that in a typical week he will have travelled thousands of miles in his large company car. Peter has always described himself as a 'happy go lucky' type; his cheerful disposition and his ability to get on well with people have been an essential part of why he has risen quickly through the ranks of all the companies he has worked for. Just lately, however, he has not been feeling himself. Little things seem to bother him in a way that they never used to, and he constantly feels 'on edge' and on a 'short fuse'. He has been irritable and moody and has found himself shouting at his wife and his children in a way that he has never done before.

His marriage has had its 'ups and downs' like many others, and they have had their fair share of arguments and fighting, but Peter has never hit his wife or his children. Similarly, while he has always enjoyed a drink, he has found himself drinking more and more lately – sometimes several glasses of whisky in an evening, and often this is the only way he can get to sleep at night. This is making him anxious because he has to be careful not to have too much alcohol in his blood when he drives the next day. Each morning he tells himself that he will only have one glass in the evening or none at all, yet when the evening comes he finds himself 'compelled' to have the first drink to settle himself, and once he has had the first one he doesn't stop.

Two recent incidents had really frightened and disturbed him. On one occasion he kicked a hole through a door at home during an argument – again, something he had never done before. More disturbing was an incident that he described as 'road rage', which occurred while driving on a long journey for work. A young driver had suddenly overtaken him at some traffic lights, and in doing so had forced him to swerve and nearly mount the pavement. Normally he would have either let such an act of stupidity pass him by, or perhaps he might have sworn at the other driver or sounded his horn in rebuke. On this occasion, he was so angered by what had happened that he chased the other driver for several miles, even though this took him off his intended route. Some minutes later, the other driver was forced to stop because of traffic and Peter got out of his car with the full intention of beating this other driver senseless. He opened the driver's car door and started shouting and swearing at him. When he saw the obvious terror in the other man's face, he realized what he was doing and was just able to stop himself from going any further. After shouting at the man he got back in his car and found himself shaking uncontrollably. The incident had scared him because he had behaved in a way that was so out of character.

When Peter eventually returned home late that night, he told his wife what had happened. She confessed that she was becoming fearful of his moods and temper and that she was getting fed up with his constant criticisms of the children and his irritability towards them. Not knowing what else to do, Peter arranged to see his family doctor and told him what had been happening. His doctor suggested he try taking antidepressants, and to this effect he was prescribed Prozac. Despite his life-long reluctance to take any medication, even for headaches, his concern about his behaviour was such that he agreed to try. Yet he insisted that he was not feeling depressed and, as such, he could not really understand why he was being prescribed an antidepressant. When he asked about this he was reassured that in any case the drugs should calm him down.

The first few weeks on Prozac were awful as he experienced nausea and an inability to get to sleep in a way in which he had not had before. In spite of this, he persevered, and continued to take the tablets he was prescribed. After several weeks he felt calmer and less irritable, though his concern about becoming dependent on the medication increased. After several months had elapsed, he decided to stop taking Prozac without consulting his doctor, and found that he still felt tense and anxious without it.

Mark

Mark met his wife when he was nineteen and she was just sixteen. She had never had a boyfriend before and, as she was unhappy at home, six months after they met they decided to get engaged, get a council flat, and to live together. At first Mark was quite attentive towards his girlfriend and he bought her presents and took her out in his car. She liked the fact that he was able to stand up to her parents and she believed that he was tough and would look after her and protect her. Soon after moving in together they got married, and it was after this that he began to be violent towards her. The first time was just a few months after they had got their flat, when he did not come home one Friday night until two in the morning. When she asked him where he had been and said that she had been worried sick about him, he flew into a blind rage and pinned her against a wall in the landing, screaming into her face. He could do what the hell he liked, he said, and who was she to tell him what he could and could not do. He was drunk and he stank of beer. She was afraid of him from that point on.

Mark started staying out and getting drunk on a more regular basis. Sometimes it would be two or three times a week and then there would be periods of a month or more without this happening. Sometimes he would stay out all night and he would be very angry with her if she showed any concern about his whereabouts. It was obvious to her that he was seeing other women, but he constantly denied this before she was even able to ask. People told her that they had seen him in town with other women. She hardly ever went out without Mark, yet despite this he was very possessive and constantly accusing her of seeing other men. On one occasion she found him following her around a supermarket, and yet he insisted that he was just there by chance and that he had not been checking up on her movements. Another time he was waiting for her after she had been out with her girlfriends. She was not back very late, but he was drunk and already in a rage by the time she got home. He punched her in the stomach and kicked at her legs. He accused her of being a 'slag' and insisted that she had been sleeping with other men. This time he really scared her for he seemed to be in a complete trance; his eyes were lifeless and he refused to see reason.

After that, she hardly ever went out in the evenings without him for fear of upsetting him. His violence grew steadily worse and he began to make sexual demands of her that she found disgusting and degrading. All the time this was happening he told her that she was ugly and stupid and useless in bed. Sometimes he would laugh at her when they were having sex. She started to become convinced that she really was ugly and that it was her fault that she was being hit. She believed that if she did what he asked of her in bed, then he would not need to see these other women. The more she tried to please her husband, the less happy he seemed to be with her. She lost a lot of weight and began to experience panic attacks and stomach cramps. Her doctor prescribed her tranquillizers when she went to see him; she did not dare mention that her husband was being violent towards her because this was his doctor as well.

At the age of nineteen she unexpectedly became pregnant. They had not been planning on having any children just yet, but Mark was never very careful and he hated using condoms. She had no idea how he would react to the news and so she kept it from him for several weeks, fearing that he would be angry with her. At times she let herself believe that it would improve their relationship and that it would mean that he might grow up and calm down. She was wrong. When she told him that she was pregnant he showed little reaction; he did not seem to be affected by the news one way or another. Three days later in another drunken state late at night he flew into a rage. She really was a 'whore' this time, and he did not believe her when she said that it was his child. He punched her in the stomach and held her down against the floor with his hand gripped tightly around her neck so that she was unable to breathe. He fumed and hissed into her face and told her that she was lying. Then he got up and left the flat and she did not hear from him for two weeks.

Out of the blue, he came back to collect some of his belongings and told her he was leaving. He had met another woman and that was the end of it. A year and a half later she saw him in town with another woman and another baby. By this time she had had her own son, but her health was bad and she needed a lot of support from Social Services after a difficult pregnancy and severe 'postnatal depression'. She was left to look after her baby on her own on state benefit, but the council rehoused her as she had a young child. She hated the area she was moved to because she did not feel safe there. Her requests to the council for a transfer never amounted to anything. Mark always denied it was his child and she was still too frightened of him to seek any money from him or report him to the Child Support Agency. She had never been close to her family but, short of money and with little alternative means of support, her mother's offer of help with her small son was not something that she could easily refuse.

·2·

Making Sense: Towards a
Social Ecology

Cultural frameworks

Each of us is born into a cultural environment that offers us
ways of making sense of our humanity that are bound by the
dominant ideologies and frameworks of the period of history
and the given culture we live in. These cultural frameworks are
constantly evolving and changing over the course of history;
sometimes they develop slowly, and at other times there are
radical shifts in the prevailing belief systems. Although we are
biological organisms driven by our physical needs, we are just
as much creatures of meaning and of culture. As such, we depend
to a much greater degree than we often realize on the collective
forms of understanding and sense-making that we are born into.
These frameworks have the potential to be liberating and illuminating, helping us to make sense of who we are, why we behave
in the ways that we do, and aiding us in our attempts to expand
our understanding of the world we live in. Cultural frameworks
can also be based on prejudice or they can be used to obscure,
mystify and confuse us. All too often, the collective frameworks
with which we try to make sense of violence and distress serve
to alienate us from our own experiences and limit our understanding of our humanity.

Violence is a part of all of our lives, whether it affects us
directly as victims, whether we know or care about others who

38

have been victimized or who have themselves been violent, whether we have lost friends or relatives through murder or violence, or simply because we are aware of violence in the world around us. This continuum of violence in society affects all of our lives in one way or another, from being careful about going out late at night, avoiding entering an empty carriage in a train, or worrying about our children on their journeys to and from school. Almost daily we read about child abuse, rape, muggings or killings, or else we see and hear the news reports on the television and radio.

Violence in all its forms – be it murder, manslaughter, rape, child abuse or the many other ways in which we are capable of brutalizing one another – fascinates, intrigues and disgusts us at one and the same time. Though we may be shocked and outraged, we are also very curious. The media focus on the seemingly bizarre, the darker, macabre side of life, has reached frenzied proportions. Films about murderers, assassins and serial killers, as well as movies packed with explicit and vivid images of death and violence, become box office successes eagerly consumed by curious millions. Not a single day passes without a film, documentary or other programme about some form of violence being shown. Book, story and film rights are negotiated even before legal conclusions have been reached: if we are not legally permitted to pay the offenders, we will pay handsomely to hear from the victims. Violence is in one form or another a great commercial success: witness the vast amount of money and time spent on the media circus that was the O. J. Simpson trial in the United States and, more recently, that of Louise Woodward, the English nanny convicted of the manslaughter of baby Matthew Eappen who died while in her care.

Perpetrators of high-profile cases become household names to be reviled and spoken of in their notoriety: Myra Hindley and Ian Brady, following the brutal sexual killing of five children in 1965, the infamous Moors murders; Peter Sutcliffe, 'The Yorkshire Ripper', who killed, maimed and attacked dozens of women in a five-year period of terror between 1975 and 1981; Beverley Allitt, 'The Angel of Death', a nurse at Grantham General Hospital who murdered four children and injured nine others in 1991 by injecting them with poisonous chemicals; Fred and Rose West, murderers of at least ten young women and girls including their own children – the terrible events at 25 Cromwell Street in Gloucester will be permanently etched on our collective memories. We will also never forget the name Dunblane, as it will now always be associated with the terrible massacre of innocent children at a nursery school. Perhaps most disturbing of all, because between them in 1993 they shattered the Western myth of the innocence of childhood, we remember the names of the eleven-year-olds Robert Thompson and Jon Venables, and their victim, two-year-old James Bulger.

What becomes central and what fascinates most of all are the questions about how and why. How could anyone do such a thing, why did one human being inflict such suffering on another? Each time there is a high-profile case, the same questions are raised and the same, often mystifying, conclusions are eventually reached. Every time such an apparently unusual or disturbing act or series of murders generate massive media coverage, all the experts are wheeled out to have their say. When all have cast their opinions into the relativistic pool that becomes the media debate, the inevitable conclusion is always reached: we 'normals' can never fully understand them, these 'others'; we will never understand why such brutal acts occur – it's incomprehensible, a mystery.

Before attempting to answer these fundamental questions and thereby to try to make sense of violent crime, it is important to note that definitions of violence and what constitutes a criminal act are not static. Just as with all forms of human conduct, the meanings ascribed to particular acts are dependent on the culture and the period of history in which they occur. During periods of war, for example, all manner of brutalities that at any other time would be defined as the worst forms of 'cold-blooded' or premeditated murder are suddenly seen as acceptable, even necessary. Indeed, during the First World War, hundreds of British soldiers were executed by their own troops for refusing to engage in killing the enemy, or because they were so traumatized that they simply were unable to. The recent war in Bosnia demonstrated how there are many crimes committed during such periods of conflict and social upheaval that have little to do with actual war: houses were looted and burnt, women and young girls were raped and killed, civilians held in captivity were murdered and tortured. Recalling the sinking of the Argentinian warship the *Belgrano* in the Falklands War as it retreated; or the haunting images at the end of the Gulf War as thousands of Iraqi soldiers were mercilessly bombarded as they queued like sitting ducks in traffic trying to go home on the Bhasra road – such events serve as a further reminder that cultural definitions of what constitutes murder, as well as what outrages people, are far from static.

Even outside periods of war, what constitutes a form of violence or murder is open to interpretation. The criminal law only defines some forms of avoidable killing as murder, and in general crime is defined so as to exclude acts committed by more powerful groups or individuals. Steven Box argues that, 'The process of law enforcement ... operates in such a way as to *conceal* crimes of the powerful against the powerless, but to *reveal* and *exaggerate* crimes of the powerless against "everyone".'[1] Who, for example, is ultimately responsible for convincing the public that turning herbivorous cattle into cannibals by feeding them animal waste products was safe, and deregulating the animal feed industry to allow this obscenity to take place? The direct result of this was to potentially poison millions of people and cause the deaths and prolonged suffering of some through Creutzfeld Jacob's Disease (CJD), the human form of BSE (Bovine Spongiform Encephalopathy). Who would be held to account if it were proven that the widespread use of organophosphates or pesticides was the cause of certain forms of neurological diseases or cancer? American car manufacturers believed it would adversely affect their sales to fit their cars with safety belts, and so they delayed doing so for decades despite the overwhelming evidence that it would save thousands of lives. Then there are the tobacco companies who for decades suppressed information about the harmful and addictive properties of tobacco; or the British firms that continued to expose their overseas employees to substances such as asbestos in factories, long after the fatal effects of those substances had been well estab-

41

lished back in Britain; the international arms dealers who legitimately sell their products to certain political regimes while knowing full well that they will be used to kill and oppress people in those countries.

Even at 'ground level' in people's direct dealings with one another, definitions of violent crime are not value-free: those who are least powerful in society are most likely to be found guilty and their actions seen as most deplorable, even if the destruction and death that they cause is minimal in comparison with institutional or more diffuse forms of corporate or political violence. Similarly, black people are massively overrepresented in prisons in Britain and North America despite the fact that the overwhelming majority of crime is committed by white people. Until recently, the majority of violent crimes against women were not taken seriously as they were seen as merely 'domestic' disputes that occurred as a normal and acceptable part of any relationship. For example, it is only recently that it has become a legal possibility for a married woman to be raped by her husband. Cases of male rape were only included for the first time in the official Home Office criminal statistics in 1997. It is still overwhelmingly the case that women in distress as a direct result of violence in their relationships are many times more likely to be referred and to receive professional help than the men who are being violent towards them. It is the women who will be in many cases defined as having an 'illness' (panic attacks, anxiety, depression) and it is they who will be medicated or receive counselling rather than the men who are being violent. Similarly, for decades children were not believed when they told of their experiences of sexual abuse: even today, many adults still find it difficult to believe that child abuse occurs to the extent that it does. The conviction rates for sexual crimes against adults, and especially children, are still only a tiny proportion of the cases that come to trial, and the cases that actually come to trial are themselves merely the tip of the rape and child abuse iceberg.

If we are to stand any chance of making sense of violent crime we have to find a way of stepping outside of the cultural frameworks that we are born into and that for the most part we do not question. There are essentially two ways we can question our commonly held beliefs and assumptions. The first is to look back at our own culture at other periods of history, and the second is to look across to other cultures. By comparing and contrasting our contemporary cultural frameworks in these ways, we might just be able to gain a fuller understanding of ourselves. Perhaps through such an endeavour we might even be able to develop new frameworks with which to elaborate and make sense of our humanity. The alternative is simply to remain constrained and thereby limited by the particular framework, bound by the culture and period of history we find ourselves living in.

Given the senseless and the increasingly brutal ways in which violent offenders are being portrayed and treated in the so-called 'developed' nations of the Western world, the need for some form of re-evaluation is perhaps more important now than ever before. The unfettered 'demonization' and the consequent hounding of people who behave violently is rapidly reaching frenzied proportions. The more horrific the offence, the more the violence shocks us and disturbs our view of humanity, so the more we seem to seek simplistic, individualistic and depersonalizing solutions to our discomfort. It is so much easier to define violent offenders as different from us, as 'other', as freaks, deviant, abnormal, sick, ill or evil.

Members of Western societies in particular are offered increasingly limited frameworks within which to try and make sense of who they are, why they feel the way they do, or why they or others behave in the ways that they do. Nowhere is this more apparent than the way in which any form of deviance is viewed. How a given culture defines some of its members as deviant is absolutely central to how that society defines its own humanity. At the same time, as we define violent people as in one way or another different from us, so we define *ourselves*. If we are to stand any chance of meaningfully making sense of why it is that some people are violent, we also need to understand why some people are not. If we are to make sense of those who are defined as 'abnormal' in whatever way, then we have to answer some very fundamental questions: how do we define

43

'madness' and how do we define 'badness'? To answer these fundamental questions might also enable us to see more clearly the destructive consequences of the way in which we have constructed our world, to prevent further violence from happening, or at least to have the possibility of stopping it getting any worse.

'Madness' and 'badness'

We do not have a common language for talking about madness or deviance that is not in some way pejorative or that allows for people in distress to be seen as essentially the same as everyone else. Thus we speak of those in distress as being 'barmy', 'doo-lally', 'nutters', 'off their heads', 'not all there', or even that they have had 'nervous breakdowns'. Even the widely accepted forms of 'mental illness' or 'mental health problems', while they do have the advantage of avoiding notions of blame (they can't help it because they are ill), define distress as 'disorders' or 'dysfunctions'. As such, this use of language and their view of distress is so pathologizing that it merely mystifies and obscures our common understanding further. More than this, the assumptions upon which the official forms of madness as 'mental illness' are made, are not only fundamentally misguided, but they are an integral part of the processes that confuse and alienate us from our own experiences when we become distressed. As such, the term that is least pejorative and that avoids pathologizing people (as much as is possible within the current frameworks) is to talk of people in or experiencing personal distress, and it is this term that I shall use throughout the book. Since we are all made of the same flesh and blood and we are, to varying degrees, shaped by the same forces, if we can make sense of our own experience of distress, then we at least have a chance of understanding how someone could be violent. The two are interconnected.

The prevailing cultural frameworks do not readily allow us to make sense of the ways in which we are altered and shaped by our experiences and the ways in which we respond to traumatic, painful or tragic events. Since we cannot readily understand why it is we become troubled or confused, we are becoming increasingly fearful of ourselves and the experiences that we have that do not readily make sense. Western cultures have increasingly defined the individual as an essentially rational, an almost self-contained biological product, somehow disconnected from all of the collective and environmental processes that help to define the self in other cultures. Individualistic frameworks seek explanations for our conduct or misconduct either within our bodies and, increasingly, within our minds. At the same time they thereby massively underestimate the impact that our material and social environment has upon us in terms of shaping who we are, how we respond to difficulties that we face during the course of our lives, and how or why we feel emotional or psychological pain.

In keeping with an emphasis on individuality and rationality, popular Western notions about sanity are very much concerned with an individual's ability to be in control, and madness as about being out of control. Thus we often hear such terms as 'pull yourself together', or 'get a grip' of yourself, as if personal distress was ultimately and essentially about internal control or the lack of it, so that to openly or visibly suffer is seen as evidence of weakness and a lack of moral strength. Those who are distressed, the 'mentally ill', have been persistently viewed and portrayed as unpredictable, incoherent, as incomprehensible and unintelligible, as irrational and too emotional, and often as potentially dangerous and therefore frightening. While we may fear 'them', those 'out there' who are violent and evil, most people also fear themselves within when it comes to trying to make sense of experiences, thoughts or feelings that are disturbing or confusing: we fear ourselves when it comes to 'going mad'. So alienated have we become from ourselves that when people experience any sign of distress this is often accompanied by a fear of losing control completely, as if they will fall off the edge of humanity and end up strait-jacketed, accompanied by men in white coats, mumbling incoherently to themselves as they pass through the gates of the local lunatic asylum. Almost every community in Britain has one such institution, and each

45

of them – like 'Bedlam' – has a name that sends collective shivers down the spine of the local population. These imposing 'out-of-town' buildings are the legacy of a Victorian era that believed in the creation of institutions to literally remove people from circulation. These places are well known to people in their surrounding communities, their names are usually whispered in hushed tones, and the fear of being admitted is matched only by the shame of having been.

Among the many prevailing myths about distress in Western societies in the late twentieth century, perhaps the most widely held and the most persistent is that people just become crazy or act violently for no apparent reason, or if there is a reason, it is because they have finally succumbed to the faulty machinery of their bodies that is their genetic fate. In other words, the most fundamental myth is the notion that violent or 'mad' people are born and not made; that there are and have been many children who have had loving, secure and happy childhoods but who subsequently became deranged and violent killers. It is a common belief that such people lead ordinary lives, then 'out of the blue' behave in an extremely irrational, incomprehensible and violent manner.

Many films and dramas have played upon the 'out of the blue' scenario, with plots about the nice person who moves in next door but isn't quite what they seem and then turns out to be a brutal and deranged murderer. There are countless cinematic representations of violent perpetrators, either as in some way possessed, soulless or evil, or as in some way mentally deranged. In either case they are portrayed in the same often mystifying and bizarre manner, with a complex but frequently unsubtle blend of the religious and the medical. Such depictions are indicative of ideological tensions within the cultural frameworks we have for understanding extreme behaviour. For as soon as we lose faith in medical explanations, then society invariably reverts to essentially religious statements about evil; we 'demonize' that which we cannot readily comprehend, and nowhere is this more so than for violent conduct. The tension between these two prevailing belief systems, the medical and the religious world-view, is so clearly illustrated by the word 'psycho', encompassing as it does both the respective polarities of 'mad' *and* 'bad'.

Despite living in an essentially secular world, our religious historical roots that defined violent offenders in terms of good and evil have not been altogether abandoned. Increasingly, violent offenders, and especially those who have committed sexual offences against children, are quite literally being viewed as in some way or another demonic: it is especially paedophiles who have become the modern-day devils in our midst. The manner in which paedophiles are being publicly identified, and then hounded across the nation from town to town, have come to resemble medieval witch-hunts rather than expressions of public concern. Similarly, crowds gathered at the trial of the child killers of James Bulger, screaming hatred, ready to attack two young boys who were seen as evil and outside of humanity. Indeed, so great was the gathered mob's collective expression of outrage, and so demonized were these boys, that some of the people outside the court felt that their own violent behaviour towards these two boys was justifiable. The role of witch-finder has been gleefully seized upon by the mass media in general and the tabloid press in particular. The media are increasingly developing the power to define reality rather than represent or report on it. The increasingly brutal and sensationalized media coverage of violent crimes serves only to fan and manipulate the flames of the most base and hateful public reactions, creating at times frenzied demonstrations – which of course then become further newsworthy items for them to consume. Any possibility of meaningful understanding or explanation within such a climate of moral condemnation and blame becomes more and more remote.

If we wish to look beyond such quasi-religious frameworks then the alternative contemporary explanations for our humanity are defined largely in terms of science – or, rather, particular versions of science. Just as in the religious domain, the scientific world also has its different faiths and denominations, none of which are as value-free or 'objective' as they would like to believe, and each with a particular view of what makes us tick. The two predominant 'scientific' ideologies are the biomedical and the psychological, both of which inform and shape our popular understanding of what it means to be human, and therefore why it is that people are distressed or violent. Indeed, these two particular ideologies have between them become *the* definitive explanatory frameworks for human conduct in Western cultures in the twentieth century. Whether it is a predominantly biological framework, or a psychological one that focuses on our individual thought processes as the primary cause of our actions, the individual reigns supreme.

Psychology

One expression of the exaggerated emphasis on the individual and on rationality is to be found in the spectacular rise of the discipline of psychology and the increasingly widespread dissemination of psychological concepts throughout popular culture. Over recent decades, how we view ourselves and how we make sense of how we function in the world has been influenced by the advent of the computer and ever-more sophisticated forms of artificial intelligence. There has been a huge proliferation of academic studies based on the 'man as machine' metaphor, and psychology departments in universities and colleges throughout Britain have steadily come to be dominated by 'cognitive' (psychological jargon for thinking) approaches to the study of our humanity. These 'cognitive' approaches are largely based on studying individual people – literally in isolation as they fill in questionnaires or as they interact with machines rather than with other people. Attention, memory, decision-making, attitudes, problem-solving and so on are all studied in individuals, all too often ignoring the fact that we *collectively* make decisions, we remember together, and we solve our problems largely with the assistance of other people. More than this, it is our ability to operate as social beings that not only precedes but actually forms the basis of the individual forms of expression we develop.[2] This emphasis on our individuality ignores the fact that we are fundamentally social beings who are defined by, and who define ourselves by, the relationships we form over the course of our lives. While it may be true that each of us has a particular way of viewing the world since each of us has unique experiences of it, it is also true that how we view the world is much more dependent on the collective frameworks we are born into and that we start to adopt as we learn to speak. It is not surprising, however, that in the age of the individual, Western cultures have taken our collective ways of making sense and reduced them to the level of individual 'perception'. Thousands of years of history and culture are altogether crammed into a particular brain and the chemistry therein.

It is as if each individual brain were a glass jar at the bottom of the river of culture. If the course of the river is the course of history, each stretch will be of a different form, speed and shape than the previous one, but still part of the same flow. While it may be true that each jar contains a uniquely different blend of stones, algae, insect life and so on, each jar also contains water from the same river. To lift a particular jar out of the river and examine its contents in isolation is to render its contents almost meaningless. To extend the metaphor a step further, to then ignore the river altogether, as so much of psychology and psychiatry is prone to do, is to discard the most important part of our humanity which is our collectivity.

While psychology focuses on the thought processes of individuals as its principal area of inquiry, these processes have now become central to the explanations that it gives for our conduct or our distress. There have been a proliferation of 'cognitive' therapeutic approaches, each stressing the primacy of our thought processes and our individual perception as the *cause* of our distress or our behaviour. Rather than viewing these individual thought processes as being directly shaped by and therefore reflecting our experience of the world, our entire world has been reduced to being constituted by these processes. In other words, it doesn't matter how malign, brutal or destructive the world you have inhabited has been, nor the tragedies or the abuses that you may have suffered, all that counts is how you *perceive* these experiences. Since each of us may perceive the same event or experience in different ways, the misguided assumption is that we can therefore pick and choose different

49

perceptions to suit our particular needs, and having done so we will start to feel a whole lot better. Rather than viewing our conduct or our distress as arising from our experiences in the world, our conduct or our distress is viewed as being *caused by* our particular thought processes, or the way in which we perceive the world. There are countless variants of this notion of 'positive thinking' to the extent that the real world has literally been reduced to an irrelevance in comparison to the all-powerful imaginary world we can invent for ourselves by thinking hard enough. Thus, for example, people who are made redundant are asked to think of the experience as an opportunity for personal development and growth rather than as a source of concern or despair. That such psychological ideas have become so popular and that the absurdity of this kind of logic is not more self-evident, is a reflection on how limited we are in the range of cultural frameworks that are available to us.

In keeping with an emphasis on individuality, the causes of our behaviour and for our distress are seen as emanating from within our bodies and especially within our heads. In this way, our individual thought processes are now widely seen as a legitimate place to look for the reasons why we behave in the way that we do. Yet it is an unmistakable truth that little of what we do is based upon rational decision-making processes and we seldom behave on the basis of pre-planned strategies, objectives or intentions. There are much more complex influences on our conduct than simply our rational decision-making processes. Much of the time our conduct is governed by our emotions and feelings which may or may not be clearly articulated, and as such we simply do not know most of the time why we feel or behave in the way that we do. We can be readily influenced by our past experiences without any conscious awareness that this is happening. Our strongest emotions are often rooted in our past experiences, whether we are consciously aware of those experiences or not and, viewed out of the historical context in which they arose, they may seen 'irrational' to others and not to make sense. Many forms of personal distress such as depression, anxiety, phobias and compulsions are simply very strong emotions that are experienced as overwhelming feelings that are beyond the individual's control. Indeed, when people become distressed in these ways, the general primacy of their emotions, as opposed to their thoughts, becomes more obvious. Such intense emotions are often a much more direct and honest reflection of the true state of our well-being than how we rationally try to tell ourselves we should be feeling or behaving. How we feel at any given time is governed not only by our past experiences, but also by powerful influences in the environment that are far beyond our ability as individuals to do much about.

In cultures that emphasize individuality and the supremacy of rational thought, it is no surprise to find that many of the claims for the differences between those who are violent and those who are not lie in the fact that violent people think differently to non-violent ones, and especially to the rest of us 'normals'. For example, that violent men perceive threat or conflict where there is 'objectively' none has been found repeatedly, or that they are often very jealous and possessive. Moir's and Jessel's book *A Mind to Crime*[3] contains many studies that apparently demonstrate psychological as well as biological differences between the violent and non-violent; countless internal, individual processes are cited as the *causes* of their violence. And given that the overwhelming majority of violent or sexual offences are committed by males, it would be stupid to deny or refute the contribution of biological or psychological factors outright.

It is certainly not my intention to ignore the contribution of individualistic factors, be they biomedical or psychological. What interests me here, though, is the way in which the relative importance of certain factors, particularly individual ones, are massively exaggerated, while other explanations are denied, obscured and hidden from view. Complex issues involving powerlessness and material as well as cultural deprivation, and their contribution to the very worst of inhumane conduct, are simplified beyond recognition. Innate nature – or rather, a grossly politicized and culturally distorted version of innate nature – is given massive prominence over environmental, material and cultural factors. The distinction between what is

51

cultural and environmental from what is biological and innate is constantly confused. Moir's and Jessel's book, despite the assertions of the authors, is full of many such individualistic distortions. Few of the many studies they cite have anything meaningful to say about the backgrounds of violent or non-violent people or the wider conditions in which the differences they display have developed. When people experience distress or behave destructively, whether as children or as adults, their distress and their behaviour is almost always a necessary and perfectly understandable *adaptation* to their environment and their experiences. In other words, much of the differences, be they biological or psychological, are signs of problems that are related to the violence and not the causes of it. Furthermore, these differences often cease to be 'abnormalities' if they can be meaningfully recontextualized; that is, when they are understood within the conditions that gave rise to those differences in the first place.

It is worth noting that the current cultural emphasis on rationality and the supremacy of our thought processes is not only reflected by psychology and psychiatry, but much of the legal system is also based upon such assumptions. For example, whether someone is convicted for having committed varying 'degrees' of murder, or whether their taking of another life is seen as manslaughter, is based on a very simplistic model of our behaviour that poorly understands the role of our emotions and our past experiences. Similarly, the widely held view that increasing the severity of punishment will act as a deterrent to violence erroneously assumes that the majority of acts of violence are in some way planned in advance . The overwhelming majority of homicides are in fact committed in circumstances of revenge, quarrel or loss of temper.

Psychiatry and the medical model

Of all the frameworks for making sense of ourselves within the language of science, the most powerful dialect is that of medicine. The medicalization of many aspects of our existence and our humanity is so entrenched that it passes largely unnoticed and unquestioned. Whether they are explicit or not, biomedical assumptions form the basis for much of how we understand ourselves. Even the ultimate moments of our existence, our entry into and departure from this world, birth and death, have been turned into essentially medical events to be controlled, administered and regulated by doctors. It is not surprising therefore that people who behave in ways that do not readily make sense, particularly those who are in extreme distress or those who behave violently, have almost without question become medicalized. Since the principal reasons for our conduct are assumed to emanate from individual biological processes, and these are seen as being controlled by our brains in some way, it follows that understanding the biochemical processes of the brain will illuminate why it is we behave or feel the way that we do.

Psychiatry is of course infused with the vested interests of huge, multi-billion-dollar drug companies who have substantial financial power with which to promote a particular view of personal distress. The psychiatric profession's insistence that it remains independent of the billion-dollar pharmaceutical industry is patently ridiculous: it is a system that is allied to and symbiotic with the drugs industry, which of course has a vested interest in promoting a biological view of personal distress and offering chemical solutions for it. The use of psychiatric medication may offer direct and pragmatic means of controlling or suppressing a person's distress or behaviour, but it has no *theoretical* validity because of this: this is not grounds for assuming that there is something biologically wrong with such people in the first place, or, if biological differences are found, that these are causes of the distress rather than its symptoms. We do not see the absence of aspirin in our bodies as the cause of our headaches simply because taking aspirin sometimes alleviates the symptoms. In any case, the efficacy of psychiatric medication in terms of anything approaching a 'cure' is so poor and so erratic that such levels would not be tolerated in any other branch of medicine. For the many patients who do get some relief from their 'symptoms', there are just as many who will not, and who instead are consigned to a never-ending experiment on their bodies in terms of different dosages of a particular drug, different types of drugs and, more typically, cocktails of all manner of drugs combined at the same time. For large numbers of patients, this experiment – which is called 'treatment' – can last for many years. There is also ample evidence that for all the often overstated benefits of psychiatric medication, the damage to patients' health in terms of a myriad of transient and permanent 'side-effects' can be profound. It could be argued that one of the advantages of a medical framework is that it does allow people to get away from the idea of blame, and especially self-blame – that he or she couldn't help it because they were 'sick'. It is a sad reflection on a society, however, that was to pathologize people in order to avoid blaming them, especially when there are forces at play influencing their actions that are far greater than any individual should be expected to cope with.

Trying to challenge the treatment emphasis of the medical model, with the economic power of the giant drugs companies on the one hand and the ideological credibility of the medical profession on the other, is like starting a game of Monopoly with only the Old Kent Road when these institutions have all the best properties with hotels on them. This alliance of biomedical interests enables one particular ideology to completely overshadow all other forms of understanding, to negate alternative explanations that point away from treatment and towards prevention, as well as to define the form and content of any treatment or help that people receive. Instead of the environment being seen as damaging, individuals themselves are implicitly defined as in some way faulty for not having survived their experiences relatively unscathed. And at the same time as the medical model individualizes personal distress, it distracts attention away from looking at the wider context in which that distress occurs. The principal emphasis of medicine, as well as most of the psychological approaches to the alleviation of distress, is largely concerned with treatment and not prevention. Imagine you are standing by a river and found that you were rescuing drowning people as they floated by, and the numbers of such people began to increase steadily, so that you found

54

yourself having to let some float by and drown in order to rescue others. Sooner or later it would be legitimate to start to ask questions about what was happening upstream and how it was that so many people were falling into the river in the first place. An emphasis on treatment would focus entirely on how best to lift people out of the river, how to do so effectively, or what forms of buoyancy aids to give them as they floated by. An emphasis on prevention would address the reasons why so many were falling in the river in the first place and why so many of them had not been shown how to swim.[4]

There have been countless radical critiques of psychiatry and the medical model being applied to people in distress, spanning back as many decades as the medical profession has been involved in 'lunacy'. Indeed, it is indicative of the massive ideological as well as economic power of the medical profession and the drugs industry as a whole that psychiatry has survived such critiques relatively unmodified. In the entire field of general psychiatry, as well as forensic psychiatry which deals with 'mentally disordered' offenders, there are enormous conceptual as well as practical problems with a medical framework.

The central role of psychiatry within many societies has always been and continues to be one of social and political control. It is equally true that some sections of the population need to be controlled for their own sake or on behalf of the rest of society, and nowhere is this more true than in the case of persistently violent offenders where the protection of the public is clearly paramount. However, psychiatry's primary function of social control is all too often confused with notions of treatment and cure that are only barely legitimate in other areas of medicine. In this way, the alleviation of distress and human suffering has been appropriated by a medical profession whose central ideology, that of individualism, has been readily borrowed in one form or another by the many other professions allied to it. This ideology has been applied with the best of intentions and motives of its practitioners, ostensibly for humanitarian reasons, and under the guise of 'treatment'. Behind the myth of scientific objectivity is always a particular prejudiced view of the world, with particular vested interests.

Psychiatric definitions of 'abnormality' in particular, under the guise of diagnostic categories of 'mental illness', have always been closely allied to the acceptable norms as defined by the most powerful groups in a given society.

The regulatory nature of psychiatry and its role as a form of political and social control is not blunted by the well-intentioned motives of practitioners or the genuine desire of many of them to help people in distress. Nor is this role negated by the personal qualities of members of the psychiatric or allied professions: it is not about them being evil or nasty people. Indeed, while I have met far too many psychiatrists who were autocratic, patronizing and completely out of touch with the realities of their patients' lives, and while the medical profession as a whole frequently remains arrogant and unaccountable, the brutalities of psychiatry and the mental health system that it dominates occur in spite of the well-intentioned motives of its practitioners. The past, however, is littered with the apparently good intentions of powerful groups defining what is in the best interests of less powerful groups, and in the process oppressing, harming or exploiting them. This has been far more transparent in other countries and in other periods of history than it is today. It was only as recently as the 1960s that homosexuality ceased to be defined as a psychiatric mental disorder which needed to be cured. This particular medical diagnosis legitimized all manner of treatments for homosexuals, some as malign as subjecting them to electric shock aversion programmes in which they were given doses of electricity for showing an interest in gay pictures. Psychiatry was closely involved in the scientific legitimization of the eugenics movement of the Third Reich in Nazi Germany.[5] It was not only Jews who were seen by the Nazis as being genetically unfit: the final solution was applied with equally fatal consequences to gypsies, homosexuals, criminals, schizophrenics, the disabled and other groups defined as biologically inferior.

Psychiatry has been used even more overtly as a system of political regulation in the communist regimes of the now fragmented Soviet Union and Eastern bloc countries; and colonial psychiatry's definitions of 'abnormality' in Africans were driven by the imperatives of subordination and based upon concepts of *normal* Africans as being inherently inferior.[6] 'The African' in the twentieth century, just as the European woman in the nineteenth century had been, was seen as being inherently unable to cope with 'civilization'.[7] As such, the history of psychiatry in colonial Africa was infused at every level with crude and racist assumptions about the nature of African subjects. One example of this, and there are countless others, is that colonial psychiatrists claimed to have established *scientifically* that there was a direct connection between the organic brain structure of the African, African psychology and African psychopathology. One of the most famous of these colonial psychiatrists, J. C. Carothers, collected 'data' which he believed demonstrated the underdevelopment of African frontal lobes; with this he constructed his theory of 'natural lobotomy', supposedly to account for the obvious intellectual and moral inferiorities of Africans: 'The resemblance of the leucotomized European patient to the primitive African is, in many ways, complete: The African, with his total lack of synthesis, must use his frontal lobes but little, and all the peculiarities of African psychiatry can be envisaged in terms of frontal idleness.'[8]

Looking back in time, the mythical status of the 'objective' standards of medical science and the prejudicial language used in medical publications seem obvious. Yet the value-laden nature of medicine and psychiatry in particular does not disappear simply because of the passage of time. The judgements that are made in the diagnosis of a particular person's 'mental illness' are therefore unlike the diagnostic judgements that are made in any other branch of medicine. Such diagnoses can never be made on the basis of objective information because there are no objective diagnostic criteria from which to come to a diagnosis, in the same way as, say, a broken leg or chickenpox. As such, there can never be complete agreement as to what constitutes the criteria for mental illnesses such as 'schizophrenia'. The assessment of any given 'mental illness' depends heavily on which particular psychiatrist (with whatever prejudices and biases that he or she holds) is making the diagnosis.[9] Any diagnosis has to be based on *how* a person interacts with and relates to the psychiatrist and, as such, any judgement the psychiatrist makes is heavily dependent on how he or she relates to the patient.

This problem does not exist anywhere else in medicine and nowhere is this more evident than when we come to the assessment of the so-called 'personality disorders'. Not only is there widespread disagreement between psychiatrists as to what constitutes psychopathic personality disorders,[10] but we also have disagreement between them as to whether such disorders are indeed 'mental illnesses' and whether they are 'treatable' or not.[11] The reliability of the diagnostic categories – that is, the consistency with which a diagnosis of an illness is made regardless of which particular psychiatrist is making the assessment – is therefore necessarily poor. Countless attempts to define particular illnesses through obsessively detailed descriptions have failed to achieve anything like acceptable levels of consistency. In any other branch of science this level of unreliability would have led by now to the abandonment of the original concept for another.

If we as a culture still readily believed in the concept of witches we would entrust the identification of them to experts, just as happened in the Middle Ages, who in turn spent endless hours devising categories and signs for the assessment of the 'witchy' personality or character. Those people (mostly women) who were defined as witches were those who did not conform (or even had been *rumoured* not to conform) in some way by their attitudes, beliefs or behaviour to whatever was defined as acceptable by the dominant religious ideology at that time. The total conviction in the belief of witchcraft allowed thousands of entirely innocent people to be denied their humanity, and to be tortured and killed for the good of the wider community. To have argued that the concept of witches was essentially meaningless and inappropriate at that time would have been seen as morally indefensible, and in itself a sign of the very same sorcery that we now accept did not exist. To argue that the concept of 'mental illness' is meaningless within a culture whose dominant ideology is convinced of the biological and genetic foundations of human distress is simply to speak with the same degree of heresy in a modern setting.

There is a widely held belief in both professional circles as

well as in popular culture that a genetic or hereditarian basis
for distress has been conclusively proven and, as we have seen,
one manifestation of this is the widely held belief that violent
people are born and not made. Yet there have been several quite
damning critiques of genetic studies and the many methodological as well as conceptual difficulties inherent in such research.
Despite the assertions of the biomedically minded, the evidence
for a genetic component to different forms of distress is nowhere
near as conclusive as we are led to believe and, where a link
has been found, the role of hereditary factors over the environment have been typically exaggerated.[12] The importance of proving a major genetic component to either distress or violence
not only has profound ideological and practical implications,
but it is also the foundation upon which a belief in the biochemical underpinning for deviance is based. Yet when we come to
consider the causes for violence, the evidence for genetics is even
weaker than elsewhere.

As Oliver James has pointed out, rates of violence vary hugely
across time and, as such, it is inconceivable that the forty-fold
increase in violence against the person in England and Wales
since 1950 could be accounted for by genetic variations.[13] In his
detailed book, James cites Carey, a biological geneticist commissioned by the American National Academy of Science, who
reviewed all the evidence for the genetic causation of violence
and who concluded that genes have not been shown to account
for even a small amount of variance between or within popu-
lations. That 'Americans are more violent than Europeans, that
black Americans are more violent than non-blacks or that some
blacks are more violent than others . . . has not been demonstrated to be even marginally explained by differences in their
genes.'[14] In his own comprehensive review of the relevant literature, including several adoption and twin studies from Sweden
and Denmark, studies into limbic functions, EEG, skin conduc-
tance, hormones and biochemistry, James concludes that, 'The
claim that the differences between violent and non-violent men
are caused by differences in any aspects of their brains or bodies
has been shown to be largely unfounded by a wide variety of
different kinds of studies.'[15]

Thus while biology may in part account for the differences found between the sexes, in that men are on the whole far more likely to be violent than women, biology cannot and does not account for differences between men who are violent and those who are not. As with the search for the precise biological underpinnings of the so-called mental illnesses, the anatomical or chemical 'holy grail' of psychiatric research has proved as elusive in the study of violence.

Decades of searching for specific biochemical correlates for distress and violence have both proved inconclusive. There will be no definitive underlying neurobiological indicators to the so-called mental illness nor to violent conduct, not only because a medical framework is largely inappropriate, but principally because the focus of inquiry is often misguided. The main causes for people's distress or their violence are to be found *outside* their bodies and not inside. I have absolutely no doubt that if we still believed in the concept of witchcraft in the way that we believe in 'mental illness' or 'schizophrenia', then there would be millions spent on identifying the gene for witchery and the biochemical mechanisms in the brain that are responsible for it. Yet much of the relentless search for abnormal neurotransmitter chemicals in the brain is based on just such cultural assumptions.

No definitive neurochemical (or indeed other biological substrates) to any of the many forms of distress have been found, despite the assertions of volumes of drug research. Nor is there any known biological substrate for psychopathy. At various times over the last five decades several different neurotransmitters and various different specific neural sites in the brain have been heralded as breakthrough discoveries in the biological understanding of all the major forms of personal distress such as depression and schizophrenia. What are merely working hypotheses are routinely presented as objective facts and indisputable scientific truths. Distress is obviously experienced as physiological events that take place in the body, in the same way as we feel any form of pain or discomfort. However, to try to locate this within specific sites in the brain seems to me to be misguided. The brain is a fantastically complex system consisting of many thousands of different chemicals and literally trillions of possible neural connections, all of which work dynamically and constantly in relation to one another, as well as to all the other processes in the rest of the body. Beyond that the brain is also a system that operates and fluctuates in response to a whole host of influences in the outside world, and in particular to other people that it has specifically evolved to be attuned to. To isolate a particular chemical out of the millions within the brain, and then similarly to pinpoint one particular area of it as the reason why people express themselves in the way that they do, is not only conceptually misguided, but is also in many cases methodologically impossible. It is the equivalent of suggesting that one particular colour, make and model of car in certain specific streets in one district of Greater London is the cause of London's traffic congestion (or even the reason for global warming). Importantly, even if consistent biochemical anomalies were found in those who are distressed or violent, this would not in any case answer the central question as to whether these biological differences are indeed inherently genetic, or if any such differences are the result of the cumulative effects of a malign environment.

At the same time, there are countless studies that have repeatedly demonstrated that familial, social and economic factors play a central role in the creation of distressed or violent children and those who become distressed or violent adults. Despite the lack of evidence for genetic or biological predispositions to violence and the vast amount of literature on the environmental causes, there is still a widely held belief in both professional circles as well as in the wider culture that people go mad or become violent (or both) because they were born in some way faulty. The psychiatric profession, and the medical model it espouses that dominates the mental health system in Britain as in so many other Western societies, systematically underestimates the importance of the events that people have experienced, the abuses they have suffered and the tragedies they have endured, and ignores the fact that these experiences in turn take place within a political, social and economic setting.

The importance of childhood and a person's overall development is poorly understood, particularly if they have had experiences that are destructive, painful or traumatic, and especially if these have taken place in their distant past. Often, little attempt is made to meaningfully link traumatic and damaging experiences in the past to the subsequent presentation of distressing thoughts, feelings or behaviours. Life experiences, no matter how damaging, are often ignored or else dismissed as only marginally relevant. Instead, 'biological mental illnesses' are seen as genetic predispositions, almost like puberty, simply waiting in the wings to blossom into fully fledged form. The premise is that, almost regardless of the life events, the biological defects or illnesses are bound to emerge and little or no further explanation is required in order to explain why someone is experiencing the distress that they are, or behaving in the way that they do. One example of this process can be seen during an initial psychiatric interview, when patients will be routinely asked if any of their relatives have had any mental illnesses. Once it has been established that a parent has a history of distress, the erroneous assumption is then made that there is a genetic link. The impact of being brought up by a parent who is distressed is ignored, as if this would not have a central role to play in the patient's development.

The more a person has suffered, then the more severe their distress or destructive behaviour will be, and yet the more likely they are to be defined as ill and their life experiences effectively ignored. In other words, the greater the actual contribution of the environment (nurture), the more likely that *nature* will be used as the explanation for their distress or their behaviour and therefore as a rationale for how best to 'treat' them. This leads to an erroneous chain of events that I will call the Psychiatric Laws of Personal Distress:

1. The more damaging the environment (past, present or both), the more extreme the forms of distress it generates will be.

2. The greater the severity of the distress, the greater the likelihood of it being seen as a medical condition.

3. The more medicalized the distress, the greater the likeli-

hood that those damaging experiences that gave rise to the
distress in the first place will be relegated to the status of
mere 'background noise' and the person in distress be seen
as having succumbed to their genetic fate.

The fact that the mental health and forensic hospital systems
are littered with clients and patients whose lives have been
afflicted by violence, abuse and tragedy is routinely ignored on a
massive scale. Complex issues involving many layers of cultural,
social, psychological, biological and material factors are reduced
to simple deterministic causalities involving individual brain
chemistry, physiology or supposed genetic abnormalities. Issues
of abuse, neglect, racism, inequality, deprivation, cruelty or tragedy are not given the prominence they deserve. Widespread
problems are removed from their context, and with the vast
majority of political and economic interests pointed towards the
treatment of 'symptoms' and the commercial exploitation of our
bodies, issues of *prevention* are swept aside. It is so much simpler
to be offered, in the form of a pill, a technical solution to the
massive political and ethical dilemmas that face us today. The
marginalization of the destructive experiences that have shaped
and formed people's distress, and the distortion of their suffering
into a biological disorder or psychological malfunction, is one
of the most brutal and widespread forms of institutionalized
violence taking place today.

The widespread and systematic failure to meaningfully assess
a person's past experience of violence or tragedy and to ignore
the impact of this is the psychological equivalent of failing to
ask a patient with breathing difficulties if they smoke; worse
still, imagine a medical approach to lung cancer that persistently
and consistently ignored the links between lung cancer and
smoking. Ignoring the direct links between the experience of
violence in all its many forms and personal distress is nothing
short of a modern tragedy. Imagine ignoring the consequences
of breathing in asbestos dust by treating hundreds of individual
patients from the same factory as individual cases of the lung
disease mesothelioma, and thereby not making any connections
between these people's working conditions and their painful

deaths. Or imagine volumes of medical textbooks that endlessly define the symptoms of cholera and typhoid, but that barely mention sanitation or water quality. Imagine a medical theory which makes little reference to fire but looks *within* the skin of a burns patient for the cause of their disfigurement.

The past is not past

Not only do the psychiatric biomedical theories obscure the ways in which we are affected by our past experiences of pain and powerlessness, but there are countless forms of therapy and counselling that serve to alienate people from their experiences as well, many of which specifically avoid delving into the past at all. I have worked with many psychologists and counsellors over the years who rarely, if ever, talk to their clients about their past experiences except to gather a 'history' of the presenting problem. While many 'cognitive' approaches seek the causes and the solutions for our conduct within our heads, many other therapeutic and counselling methods are only really concerned with the present and the future. As with the psychiatric model, such problem-solving or 'symptom management' approaches all too often treat the forms of distress they encounter as meaningless symptoms to be removed or controlled, rather than as legitimate forms of experience to be accepted, understood and validated.

All too often counselling and therapy are administered as technical solutions to moral problems in exactly the same way as tablets are prescribed. These psychological approaches have done as much to obscure the effects of a malign environment as has psychiatry. More than this, these ideas feed into and are reflected by the wider culture so that they become part of the fabric of our general understanding of ourselves. Thus there are many forms of expression of the philosophy of not dwelling on the past: 'what is past is past', 'what is done is done', 'water under the bridge'. While these sentiments are often meant to be helpful, they ignore the embodied nature of our past experiences and the fact that people who are distressed cannot forget or ignore their distress any more than they can stop breathing.

There are personal as well as social reasons why we are prevented from discovering the true extent of our inhumanity and maltreatment of each other. Victims themselves, whether as children or adults, often do their best to forget what they have been through and avoid talking about their experiences because to do so is painful and difficult. As a sign of our increasing alienation from our distress, any attempt they might make to talk about traumatic experiences often leaves other people feeling awkward and embarrassed. Friends or relatives are often fearful that because they are not trained experts, they will only make matters worse, so that even our most basic forms of compassion and understanding for each other are now seen as specialized professional skills. Often victims will not have told anyone what has actually happened to them because they are ashamed of what they have been through, or else blame themselves in some way. Also, they may be convinced that they will not be believed (this is in fact often the case) or else that they will be judged harshly by others. Disclosures of abuse, domestic violence, rape or sexual harassment are still all too often seen as an 'excuse' or else as entirely made-up fiction.

There is also a widespread view that to take into account someone's past experience of abuse or violence is an excuse that merely lets them avoid responsibility for their conduct, especially if that person has been violent themselves. Increasingly, the only place for victims of violence to give accounts of their experiences is in the isolated environment of the therapy room where, if the victim is fortunate, the therapist will recognize the signs, be bold enough to ask the right questions, and compassionate enough to be a witness to the realities of what that person has been through.

No matter how terrible or brutal people's experiences have been, especially during childhood, it is very rare for them as adults to see those experiences as in any way different from anyone else's. After all, each of us has only experienced our own childhood and we cannot readily make comparisons with other people, even if they have grown up in the same family. A clinician and therapist in my position, however, who has bothered to find out about people's past histories, may have privileged access to literally thousands of different childhoods from which to compare and contrast. When you have heard about countless childhoods and the different forms of abuse and tragedy, patterns begin to emerge: certain forms of abuse, combinations of abuse, or even childhood tragedy lead to particular expressions of personality or particular forms of distress. The one flows inexorably from the other, as surely as night follows day. When faced with a patient with long-standing personal or social difficulties, or who is experiencing severe distress, it is not a case of *whether* something destructive or painful has happened to them but *what*. The form that their personality or their distress has taken points obviously backwards in time and offers clues as to the kind of experiences that have shaped the difficulties the person has been struggling with.

The fact that distress has become so medicalized means that the main way people have for making sense of their experiences is through a framework of symptoms and illnesses and their first point of call will be their doctor. Despite the attempts of the medical profession and those working in the mental health field, the public remain unconvinced that forms of distress are just like any other illnesses. What is so unfortunate, however, is that their justified sense of the inadequacies of the medical model is replaced instead by an essentially moralistic framework that is based on personal weakness of 'character'. There is still an enormous amount of stigma about being distressed, and behind this stigma are thinly veiled assumptions about moral or personal failing. Almost all of the people I have seen over many years in my consulting room have arrived heavily burdened with shame for being distressed. With very few exceptions, they are convinced that their suffering is an indication of personal weakness rather than a necessary response and adaptation to a painful world. No matter how awful or hideous or terrible the experiences and ordeals they have been through, no matter the extent of the blatant exploitation or violence in their relationships, they almost always make no connection between what they have been through and their current distress. No matter how brutal or destructive their experiences have been, they are persistently dogged by the conviction that their distress is an indication that they have failed in some way to cope. This view will only too readily be reinforced, however implicitly, by so many of their friends and relatives. Most unfortunate of all is the fact that there is a whole array of mental health services that will devalue their experiences, render them irrelevant and – albeit unwittingly, and with the best of intentions – reinforce the view that there is something fundamentally abnormal about them.

Towards a social ecology

The cultural frameworks that are available today simply do not make it easy to understand the ways in which we as individuals are shaped and influenced by events that lie beyond our bodies, least of all those that have occurred in the distant past. The way each of us perceives the world and feels about ourselves is based on our experiences of the world and especially of other people in it. Contrary to the current emphasis on individuality, the relationships we form throughout our lives, from the minute we enter this world, form an integral part of who we are as well as how we are. Our personal relationships with others are our reference points; we define ourselves and are defined by them. If we are to understand why it is that we become distressed or why it is that some of us become violent, we need to take into account our personal histories and the past relationships that we have had, in addition to what is happening in the present.

More than this, our humanity cannot be reduced simply to the biology of our bodies or the processes of our individual minds. We are complex creatures that need to be understood as products of social, cultural, economic, ecological and political influences as well as psychological and biological processes. What is required is a shift away from viewing our bodies as contained biological units and looking constantly *inwards* for the causes and explanations for our dis-ease, our distress or our conduct. We are slowly as a species becoming aware that we are part of a much greater ecology and the insights from the environmental movement have highlighted that the health (indeed, the survival) of individual organisms depends almost entirely on the ecology of the environment they occupy. What we require, therefore, is a way of making sense of our health and our conduct that looks outwards rather than inwards, away from our bodies and individual biology, and instead towards the relationships we form and the environment that those relationships take place in. We may be biological organisms that are influenced by the physical environment in which we live, but just as importantly we are social creatures who are hugely dependent on other people for our survival. This is what lies at the heart of a social ecology in which our relationships, both past and present, take centre stage. And just as relationships have the potential to be sustaining and supportive, they can also be destructive and damaging – and nowhere is this more so than in relationships that are in some way violent or abusive.

We can fight, compete or co-operate with one another. We can exploit and manipulate each other, or we can assist and enable. We can obstruct each other's progress through life or we can encourage each other along the way. We can support or look after those who are less fortunate than ourselves or we can ignore them. The way in which a given society is structured profoundly influences the kinds of relationships that are formed and whether particular forms of relationship are encouraged or suppressed. If we are to understand our relationships, and why some of them become destructive, then we need to understand our social ecology. That is, we need to make some reference to the global social climate, to the wider context in which relationships are embedded. There is a growing recognition that rates of consumption, pollution and environmental degradation by the industrialized world have become unsustainable and that the consequences for our global ecology have been disastrous and could potentially be catastrophic. Likewise, there have been equivalent changes that have been happening to our social ecology, rendering many relationships unsustainable, and with widespread consequences for our health and for increasing levels of violence in society.

An ecological approach to our humanity, our health and our

conduct recognizes that we are profoundly shaped by our social and political environment. Such an analysis may enable our attention to be focused on prevention and not simply treatment. The greatest advances in public health have not been achieved through the treatment of individuals, but by actively seeking out and eliminating the conditions that gave rise to widespread suffering and human mortality. Cholera and typhoid were not eradicated by endlessly treating the individual sufferers of these diseases, but by actively seeking out the conditions that created them, and then spending vast sums of public money on eliminating those conditions by providing widescale systems of sanitation.

We need an ecological understanding of both our health and our conduct that allows people's experiences throughout the course of their lives to take centre stage, so that the impact of their social as well as their material environment can be taken fully into account. One where events and happenings that lie well beyond the control of the individual are given their due consideration; where people's abilities to cope and the limits of their abilities to do so, their vulnerabilities, their anxieties and fears, and their frailties are all seen to be shaped first and foremost by the experiences they have had. The extent to which we experience personal distress in whatever form is directly related to the extent to which the world that we occupy harms us. The earlier that painful or destructive influences play a part in the development of our personalities, the more damaging and more enduring their consequences become. The extent to which we express ourselves through violent conduct is *directly related* to the extent to which we have experienced violence. What is remarkable at this very late stage of the twentieth century is that these simple truths are still being obscured.

In society today, people are too readily persuaded that when they are unwell or are suffering it is because there is 'something wrong' with them; that no matter how terrible or destructive the social ecology they have been in or continue to inhabit, their suffering is either as a result of their faulty biological make-up, their lack of moral fibre, their 'attitude', or because they are like that out of choice. For increasing numbers of people in society, their social environment has become completely unsustainable, with profound consequences for the relationships that they grow up in and that they form as adults. Unsustainable forms of social organization that have been developed this century are increasingly being adopted on a global scale as we approach the millennium. The nature of that unsustainable social ecology, as well as the inevitable widespread degradation that it creates, is the focus of Chapter 6.

·3·

The Past and Future: The Legacy of Child Abuse

Personal distress and violence are opposite sides of the same coin; they are closely and often inextricably linked. Violence and distress, in whatever form they take, are ultimately about power and control and both can be seen as an expression of powerlessness and a lack of control. The experience of powerlessness is the basis for the overwhelming majority of 'mental health problems' and it is this experience that is the basis for most acts of violence. People become distressed, harm themselves or others because of what has happened to them. Distress or violence arise as a direct result of painful and destructive experiences that people have over the course of their lifetimes, experiences over which they typically have had little or no control. When personal distress is experienced as a more or less persistent feature of a person's life,[1] or when people express themselves through behaving violently, invariably their distress or violence originates from tragic or traumatic childhood experiences. Most of those destructive experiences occur in the form of violence expressed as child abuse and neglect.

The strategies that people adopt to cope with such violence are attempts to regain a sense of control over their lives and thereby to counter the experience of powerlessness that is so much an integral feature of child maltreatment. Adaptations to childhood maltreatment and the forms of distress and behaviour that this creates are wide-ranging and multifaceted. They may be

71

expressed at the time, persistently over the course of a lifetime, or many years later in adulthood. These adaptations may ultimately prove to be self-defeating, destructive or violent, but they are adaptations for coping none the less and they have almost without exception developed for perfectly valid and understandable reasons. Once a person's distress or violent conduct is placed back within its original context, then its form and content start to make sense once more, for only then can it meaningfully be seen as an understandable response to malign experience. The particular form in which people's distress or violence manifests itself is seldom random. Invariably, the form that it takes is shaped by the conditions and experiences out of which the distress or violence originally developed and to which it was an adaptation.

No matter how old we are, we do not become immune from being shaped and affected by whatever misfortune or tragedy befalls us. Experiencing events and situations that harm us and that are beyond our control will have an impact on our health and personality regardless of our age. All of the processes, responses and adaptations that are involved in child abuse and neglect apply equally to adult victims of violence. That violence may occur in the form of 'domestic' violence, repeated rape within a relationship or on one occasion only, or in the form of physical or emotional assault. Much of what follows on child abuse could therefore equally apply to adult victims of violence or tragedy, yet the extreme differences in relative power between adults and children mean that when children are involved the experience is often magnified tenfold, as are the potential consequences; in childhood, such experiences are *developmental*; that is, they are experiences that profoundly shape the development of a child's personality or character.

The earliest experiences that we have, particularly in the first ten or so years of life, are without doubt the most important in terms of setting the foundations upon which our personalities are subsequently built. Self-confidence, self-worth and self-esteem are not merely empty psychological words, they relate to the way in which we view ourselves, how we see ourselves in relation to other people, the world we inhabit and our place in it. All these are to a large degree formed and shaped by our experiences in these early years. Our past relationships, especially the very first ones we experience, provide the blueprint for the kinds of relationships we subsequently form and how we as adults later relate to other people. Whether we were wanted as children, whether we were supported, encouraged and loved, will all have a massive bearing on how we subsequently view ourselves and whether or not we view the world as a safe and caring place to inhabit. The family has traditionally been portrayed as the most basic and fundamental place of security, safety and belonging, yet for so many people experiences of family life and early relationships fall far short of this mark. If in the crucial formative years we are denied love, if we are unwanted, neglected, rejected, stifled, exploited or beaten, or if the relationships that we form with others are damaging, controlling or uncaring in some way, all this will set the stage for an almost unshakeable view that we are worthless and unlovable and that the world is an unsafe, unpredictable and frightening place to be. If the formative years of a person's character are based upon the uncertainty and threat that are such an integral part of child abuse, then these experiences, in the absence of any mitigating love and support, will become more or less 'built in' to a personality. These are the experiences that lay the foundations for all the forms of distress that are known as 'mental disorders', as well as for violence.

Violent childhood experiences are necessary for creating a potential predisposition to subsequent violent behaviour. Each of the principal forms of child maltreatment – that is, physical, sexual, emotional abuse or neglect – can have distinct ramifications for children and the development of their personalities. However, since each form also involves the experience of powerlessness, they also have common features in terms of their impact on children. Of all of the ways in which children can be harmed, it is physical and sexual abuse that are most readily defined as violent, and without doubt it is these forms of abuse in particular that have the most destructive consequences. However, it is rare for a child to be maltreated in one way alone, physical and sexual abuse, for example, necessarily contain within them elements of

73

emotional abuse as well. More than this, child maltreatment often occurs within relationships that are characterized by persistent fear and continual tension, and this can take place over many years. There are, of course, children who are abused in *all* possible ways, either by the same person, or in different ways by different people at different times over the course of their childhoods and into their adult lives.

It is important to stress that the *intent* of the adults who harm children is irrelevant here, what really matters are the consequences of their actions for those children, either at the time or for many years subsequently. It is possible to mean well and yet to act in ways that result in quite the opposite being achieved. Paedophiles can and often do insist that their sexual exploitation of children was done lovingly, that they did not *intend* to cause harm. Many parents control, humiliate and beat their children with the best of motives and with the *intent* of bringing them up in the best possible way. Similarly, I have worked with many adults who as children grew up in religious institutions that inflicted the most vicious and brutal regimes on them, almost invariably justified by a twisted moral imperative that deems such treatment wholly appropriate, *for the children's benefit.*

There are also many other childhood experiences that, though they may be tragic and painful, could not be described as inherently abusive or violent – such as the death of one or both parents or parental separation. None the less, such experiences can also have an adverse impact on children and their development. While it is important to clarify the different forms of child maltreatment and the consequences each one can have, it is often the cumulative effects of many destructive experiences that need to be understood in order to make sense of why people eventually come to express themselves in brutal ways.

Sexual abuse

There are a great many misconceptions about what constitutes sexual abuse, the most persistent being that 'sexual' equates with sexual intercourse. There are, of course, many other ways in which children can be sexually abused without involving genital penetration; for example, the penetration may be oral or anal instead. In addition, there are many forms of abuse in which the adult or older child carrying out the abuse may not commit any act of penetration at all. For example, the child may be asked to touch the abuser, or the abuser may masturbate against or on top of the child (or with the child on top of them) without necessarily even undressing. While many people are familiar with the sexual offence of 'flashing' in which an adult male exposes his genitals, many people are surprised to discover that children can be sexually exploited in ways that do not actually involve bodily contact at all. An obvious example of 'non-contact' sexual abuse would be the photographing or filming of children naked or in sexually suggestive poses or activities, either on their own or with other adults, children or animals. Children may be made to abuse each other or to watch while other children are being abused. They may also be made to watch sexually explicit films or to inappropriately witness adults involved in sexual activity, whether the adults involved are consenting to that activity or not. For example, I have worked with several adults who as children witnessed their mothers being raped by their partners.

Other misconceptions surrounding the sexual exploitation of children is that they are in some way raped or 'forced' when being abused. While some abusers do indeed employ physical violence, this is in fact only rarely the case. Children are often manipulated and deceived in ways that do not involve the use of physical coercion. In many cases, the threat of punishment, violence or rejection may be sufficient to frighten the child into passive compliance and to maintain their subsequent silence. Such threats may be made either prior to the abuse, while it is happening, or after it has stopped. Children may be told, for example, that if they don't do what is requested of them they will be permanently sent away or even killed. Similar threats may also be made if they tell anyone what has happened or what is still happening to them. They may be blamed or held responsible for the abuse and therefore feel that it is they who will be in trouble if anyone discovers what is happening. Even just the vague sense that they are involved in something that is wrong or bad can keep children in silence.

Children, just like all of us, are fundamentally social animals. They depend entirely on the adults around them for their survival for a period of time longer than for any other species on earth. While these social imperatives have enormous advantages in terms of the potential for learning and for the transmission of culture from one generation to the next, it also makes them very susceptible to exploitation and manipulation. Young children need and depend on physical contact with those around them; indeed, that is the way they have evolved, and as such are programmed to seek out and to respond to social cues and stimuli from the moment they are born. This need for physical contact has been distorted into sexual proclivity not only by those offenders who seek to exploit them, but by a whole host of so-called 'experts' of child development as well as therapists from Freud right up until the present day.[2] While children need and thrive upon physical contact and sensual stimulation, they are *not* sexually aware, and to attribute sexual instincts to their displays of physical intimacy is a profound misconception. They may derive pleasure from all forms of touching, including genital stimulation, but we should not attribute sexuality to this any more than we should when they derive pleasure from other forms of stimulation such as being hugged, or stroked on other parts of their bodies such as their heads or faces. Neither does it make any biological sense for children to have any form of meaningful sexuality until they have reached puberty. While some children who are sexually abused can experience pleasure or enjoyment from certain aspects of what is done to them, such as being cuddled, kissed or caressed, this has far more to do with their need for physical contact and sensual stimulation than anything to do with their supposed sexuality. They may be able to mimic and simulate sexualized behaviours, particularly when they have been subjected to these during abuse, but again this does not have the same meaning as for adults.

For children who are in some way unwanted or unloved, who have experienced rejection or other forms of emotional or physical abuse, the need to be loved and to have tactile affirmation of this can override whatever pain, confusion or discomfort they may experience during or after the episodes of abuse. Children who have been rejected, neglected or otherwise denied love are all too frequently the ones who are also sexually exploited. No matter how intense the discomfort, children may well believe that their abuse is love, that this distortion of intimacy is not a perversion. In fact, it may seem to them that someone is giving them their undivided attention, which they may not have received elsewhere. Some sexually abused children learn that the only form of intimacy and seemingly benign attention that they can receive is through being sexually exploited. Children's need for physical contact and sensual stimulation enables perpetrators to manipulate young children into situations that they then sexualize, and without the need for physical violence, threats or coercion. Psychologists have given this process of manipulation the rather distasteful term 'grooming'. The overwhelming majority of cases of sexual abuse take place by perpetrators who are in one way or another known to the child and therefore the abuse takes place in the context of a relationship that already exists. For the most part, children have to be isolated and the abuse needs to take place in a private location with the minimal chance of being caught or discovered by others. What begins as acceptable public intimacies such as hugging, holding hands or sitting on knees is sometimes suddenly, but more usually systematically and gradually, transformed into private acts that are for the sexual pleasure of the perpetrator. The usual physical boundaries of relationships between adults and children are distorted to an end that only one party knows about and only one party can ever fully understand.

Once the contact becomes sexual, children typically experience a great deal of confusion as they literally have no way of making sense of what is happening. They may be experiencing a great deal of physical pain or be terrified, they may not be able to breathe, or they may be overwhelmed by repulsive and unfamiliar smells. They may be choking or forced to swallow ejaculate or wipe it from their faces or bodies, and yet at the same time they are either told that they are loved or even that they are bad. They may be reassured that what is happening is an acceptable part of loving them and that they are special. Once the episode of abuse is over, they may then be rewarded by being given sweets or gifts that other children do not receive, which then reaffirms that the relationship is a special one. The continued appropriate and often public displays of affection from the perpetrator may serve to confuse the child even further. More than that, however, such open displays will often affirm to others that the relationship is indeed a special and close one.

There are many factors preventing a disclosure of sexual abuse either at the time it is happening or for many years after. Threats of harm or punishment made by the perpetrator are believed – after all, children have no reason to doubt the word of an adult and no way of knowing whether or not any threats will be carried out. The most consistent reason children keep quiet, however, is the universal tendency for victims to blame themselves for the abuse and to feel responsible for what is happening to them. In addition, children often find the experience of abuse confusing as well as frightening, and though they may have a sense that the abuse is wrong they do not often understand why or what is being done to them. If they are very young their verbal skills may still be poorly developed, and so they often have very limited ways available to them for expressing what is happening. The child may fear the consequences of a disclosure if they are aware that this may lead to family discord or break-up, or the perpetrator being sent away to prison. Since they are usually in a relationship with the perpetrator, they may well have very many other conflicting emotions towards them as well as wanting the abuse to end. In any case, the child assumes in most cases (usually quite accurately) that if they did tell anyone what was happening they would not be believed. The difference in power and status between the child and the perpetrator, the fact that the abuse is often hidden from view with no tangible evidence or witnesses, means that it is the child's word against an adult's. Despite the many studies that now indicate the widespread prevalence of sexual abuse in many Western countries, it is still all too often the case that an adult will be believed more than a child. The younger or the more

handicapped the child, the less the likelihood that their disclosures will result in any legal action.

As well as the inherent difficulties in proving such concealed
violence, the legal processes that might lead to some form of
redress are themselves hopelessly inadequate, with only a tiny
amount of cases reaching court and a fraction of these ever
finding in favour of the child. Similarly, I have worked with
many adults whose disclosure of sexual abuse as a child was
met with physical punishment, further sexual abuse or complete
disbelief, thereby brutally affirming the silence that they dared
to try and break. Children may well have no one in their lives
whom they can trust to tell in any case, as there are children
who are abused, rejected and neglected by all of the important
adults in their lives.

Physical abuse

Discussions about what constitutes physical abuse of children
are hampered by a complete confusion as to what constitutes
'acceptable' levels of violence in child-rearing. What some
people consider a mere 'smacking' would be to other observers
a brutal and violent beating. Whenever the use of violence as a
means of controlling or chastising children is discussed, this
problem of definition emerges without anyone either honestly
declaring the actual levels of violence they employ, or else using
the same terms as each other but actually referring to quite
different degrees of violence. To add to the confusion, there are
both cultural and class differences that are deeply embedded in
terms of what constitutes appropriate levels of physical punishment of children, all of which are highly associated with ever-
shifting notions of childhood and child development. Regardless
of the unsupportive views of some child development experts,
and with the encouragement of yet others in this field, the use
of some form of violence to control children is generally not
only seen as acceptable, but the unquestionable prerogative of
parents. It was only as recently as 1986 that the British government made the use of corporal punishment illegal in state schools

in Britain, and yet fee-paying parents still retain the right to allow their children to be beaten in private schools. To state that any form of violence towards children is unnecessary and inappropriate, or that it merely teaches children harsh lessons about brutal forms of domination and control through fear rather than respect, or even that there are many far more effective forms of teaching children and shaping their behaviour other than through hitting them – in many sections of society – will almost certainly fall on deaf ears. Various levels of hitting, shaking, shoving and pulling children is for much of the population an acceptable method of child-rearing and will remain so.

The more extreme forms of physical violence against children are not debatable. When they are beaten, vigorously shaken, thrown around, pinned against a wall by their throats, poisoned, burnt and scalded, or stabbed with sharp objects, we do not have a problem recognizing it as abuse. However, the transition between physical punishment and physical abuse is a much finer one and is as much about the manner as well as the severity of the violence employed. It is clear that those parents who abuse their children physically do so in a chaotic manner that is not linked to the child's behaviour. Typically they do so out of their own irritability and frustration, their need to be in control of others, and some even out of the enjoyment that this easy form of power brings them. In other words, the 'punishment' is typically an expression of the adult's inability to cope and serves no purpose in terms of altering the child's behaviour. More than this, the violence usually takes place in emotionally abusive environments as well, where the child is frequently or constantly reprimanded or scolded. Threats of smacking or punishment are applied completely inconsistently or not at all. Many of the attacks are 'unprovoked', and on the basis of the abuser perceiving malevolent *intent* in the child or blaming them for things they have or have not done, or are supposed to have done. Appropriate behaviour is neither modelled nor praised.

The experience of violence or abuse need not be direct, but can be quite vicarious: many children suffer the consequences of watching their parents' violence towards one another, their acrimonious shouting and arguing, or through witnessing physical or sexual assaults on others within the family. Parental discord, regardless of whether it is in the form of constant rowing or domestic violence or whether that violence is directly aimed at the children or not, can certainly be damaging to offspring. Even households in which the adults' relationship with one another is violent or destructive, but which is relatively concealed, can and usually does affect the children. The emotional tensions in the home are all too readily picked up by others in the house and the adults' own distress will directly influence the quality of the relationships they have with the children. Such emotionally charged atmospheres can last several years or even the entire duration of a person's childhood.

Emotional abuse

There are, of course, other ways in which children can be maltreated that can also have devastating long-term consequences. The ways in which adults can be cruel and brutal to children (and, of course, to each other) are almost limitless, and I am no longer surprised by the different and varied forms that I hear in my clinics. Though emotional abuse often accompanies other forms of abuse (and other forms of abuse are, by their very nature, emotionally abusive as well), it is characterized as much by what is done or said as by what is not. Adults can be vicious and brutal towards children without ever touching them, and in many cases the *threat* of something being done is just as terrorizing as it actually happening. For example, the child may have a knife held to its throat or else it may be threatened with harm either to itself or to a favoured toy or pet. For young children in particular, the use of excessive shouting can be terrifying in itself, and abusive parents can be seen in public places towering over their children and screaming into their faces.

Children may be denigrated through verbal cruelty, taunting or derogatory name-calling, or by frequently being reminded that they were not wanted. They may be constantly compared unfavourably to someone else, usually a sibling, or routinely criticized or blamed for anything that goes wrong. Children may be put down or humiliated in front of others; for example, I worked with a man who from the age of five had a dog collar routinely put on him and who was made to eat his food on the kitchen floor in front of his siblings while the family barked mockingly at him. As well as regular criticism or disapproval of whatever they do or say, children may be reminded of their mistakes or else have their achievements ignored or minimalized. In a local pet shop recently, I watched as a middle-aged woman told what I took to be her ten-year-old son what he should and should not be doing. Over a ten-minute period and almost without catching her breath, she alternated between telling him exactly what to do, her voice getting louder and louder until he did so, and then almost as soon as he had done what he had been told to, she scolded him for not doing it correctly. Children may be regularly ascribed attributes that clearly do not belong to them or that belong to other people: being told you are selfish, driven by jealousy, bad or evil or that you are 'just like your father' (who was a violent drunk but is now absent). They may be locked in cupboards, coal sheds or their bedrooms, or left on their own for periods of time to look after themselves.

Having the sole responsibility of looking after yourself, or younger siblings (this is usually the fate of the eldest child) or of a sick parent or relative at too young an age, can also be detrimental. This often happens to children whose parents have a chronic health problem (of whatever kind) or those whose parents are routinely drunk. Such parents may refuse to seek other forms of help, insisting on only the particular child in question caring for them. Children can be isolated in other ways too; for example, by being prevented from seeing or playing with their friends or from forming any relationships outside of the immediate family.

One of the most destructive forms of emotional abuse is through the highly conditional provision of love (entirely on the carer's terms or when the child acts exactly as the adult wants them to) or through its withdrawal or denial. Rejection can be used in a way that is systematic and punitive, especially when the child is completely ignored as the adult withdraws into prolonged periods of cold, empty silences. Rejection can also be a permanent feature of the relationship in the form of never giving the child any emotional warmth or physical affection. This may happen only towards a particular child, leaving that child with little doubt about his or her differential status. The selective use of material rewards is not restricted to the sexual exploitation of children. Children can also be emotionally abused and manipulated through the controlled use of money or material gifts. They can be rewarded for behaviour that is acceptable to those in control of the purse strings, and conversely they can be punished by the withdrawal of those rewards. While all of this can be carried out with apparently the best interests of the child in mind, and this may be a widely used method for encouraging children's development in an increasingly materialistic world, it can also be carried out cruelly and coercively.

Neglect

There are many ways children can be neglected and not taken care of adequately. The most basic forms of neglect involve not attending to children's physical needs. Children may be given inadequate amounts of food, or food that is insufficiently nutritious, or they may not be kept warm enough through insufficient clothing. Alternatively, they may be kept too hot through too much clothing, or put in clothes that are unsuitable for their age or size, for example, being kept in shoes that are far too small for their growing feet. The basic need for cleanliness may be unattended to, so that they are not washed or are kept in dirty clothes, or they may live in or be fed in unhygienic conditions. Failure to ensure that children receive adequate medical attention is another form of neglect. The treatment they require but do not receive may be for life-threatening conditions, as well as less serious problems such as head lice. Just as important as their basic physical needs, neglected children may be left unattended for long periods of time without the social stimulation they need in order to develop.

As well as the inadequate provision of food or social contact, there are of course other ways in which carers can neglect their responsibilities and thereby allow harm to come to children through failing to act rather than through their actions. Adults may, for example, leave sharp knives, syringes or medication where children can easily reach them, or leave windows open where they might fall out. Children can also be quite literally abandoned by one or more of their carers. For example, by being left alone or left behind, by being sent away or moved from one carer or relative to another. At the severe end of neglect, young children who are denied adequate social contact and stimulation, as well as material sustenance, can literally give up on life, stop eating, and eventually die. This is known as 'non-organic failure to thrive'.

Separation and divorce

There are other conditions of uncertainty that may have adverse effects on children. Separation and divorce are often deeply disturbing for all parties involved but especially for children, regardless of how acrimonious or destructive the original household was or how smoothly or amicably the separation or divorce. Many children are often left with feelings of rejection and insecurity. Since their parents' relationship is the very first and most basic one they encounter, they often develop a sense that all meaningful relationships are characterized by discord, instability and impermanence. All too often, divorce and separation occur within continued acrimony and hostility, the emotional ramifications of which are quickly picked up on by the children involved. The parents themselves, particularly mothers to whom the continuing care of the children will generally fall, will frequently be more irritable, distressed, tired and generally less available for their children during this period than if they were in relatively stable and supportive relationships. The children are often placed in unfamiliar and confusing situations as they become caught between the separating parties and they have to negotiate the emotional minefield of divided loyalties that ensues. This confusing state of conflict and tension may continue long after the actual period of transition and separation has occurred.

There are typically many structural changes to the household in terms of people leaving and arriving, and possibly changes in living conditions or standards as well. In addition to the upheaval and uncertainty that these changes bring, there are further complications in terms of the processes involved when families merge into step-families with the arrival of unrelated adults and children. Step-parents and step-children find themselves trying to relate to one another without any clear sense of how this is supposed to happen. There are no guidelines, no clear sense of responsibility, duty or moral codes between step-relatives, and as such they may end up relating to one another not only with confusion but sometimes with hatred and intolerance as well. Many step-parents have very different notions as to how their children should be brought up, resent their partner's ways of dealing with their own children, and may treat their step-children with far less tolerance than their own. It is sadly all too common for abuse and cruelty to take place in situations where adults and children who are not related to one another are living together in close proximity. It may well be that clinicians such as myself only see the consequences of step-parents and step-families that have been cruel, destructive or violent. Yet so often is this the case that it does highlight the potential fragility of this increasingly widespread form of social organization, especially when it is characterized by continued instability and constant change.

Children of chaos

There are an increasing number of children whose lives are characterized by instability, neglect and violence. They cannot be said to belong to any discernible family either because their family structure is constantly changing, because they are constantly being looked after by different people, or simply because there is no family unit at all. Their lives are quite literally chaos. Over the course of their lives many of these children will have been subjected to all forms of child abuse and neglect. They will more often than not have been physically and sexually abused from a very young age, and they are likely to have witnessed high levels of violence to their mothers or siblings. Typically their fathers will be completely absent, or else barely in contact such that they will have had little or no contact with their children. Any other male figures in these children's lives will tend to be transient; for example, their mother's lovers who move in, live with them for a time, and then leave as quickly as they came. Some of these men will continue the pattern of violence, either in terms of being physically or verbally aggressive, or they may even be sexually abusive towards one or more of the children as well.

The mothers in these family set-ups are likely to have had several children, each by a different father. Such mothers may alternate from neglecting the children and leaving them unsupervised for much of the time, to periods of crisis whereby they can no longer cope with their children's behaviour. If they come to the attention of Social Services, some or all of these children may well be taken away from their mothers because they are unable to be cared for adequately at home, or because the levels of violence or abuse at home has put the children at too great a risk of harm. As such, many of these children will at some stage be 'in care', either in a residential unit or through the fostering system. This move will either be temporary, with the children moving in and out of the care system and back again, or more permanent, whereby the children are removed from their homes completely. In either case, they may or may not maintain contact with their biological parents or what is left of their original family. Each change in the household, and each move in and out of care or to different foster parents, will of course be accompanied by uncertainty, insecurity, rejection and abandonment. These are the children of chaos, and their fate is very much the focus of Chapter 5.

The legacy of abuse

As creatures of meaning we need to have a sense of stability and order, a sense that the world is at least predictable enough for us to be able to operate effectively in it and to feel reasonably in control of our lives. Though any assumption of stability is largely illusory (the unexpected death of a loved one or natural disasters are evidence enough of that), none the less we operate in a world in which we create for ourselves a sense of predictability. Conversely, we do not tolerate prolonged uncertainty at all well, and if there is one thing we tolerate even less than this it is uncertainty combined with threat over which we have no control. Torturers know this only too well and put this to good effect: one minute you are being beaten, the next looked after. One minute deprived of sleep, the next permitted to do so. More often than not it is this total unpredictability and the control of the torturer that destroys people rather than the actual physical pain itself.

As much as children need food, water and the benign love and attention of those who care for them, from the minute they are born they also require a world that is relatively predictable. All forms of childhood maltreatment occur within a context of relative powerlessness for the child, which is characterized by a more or less complete lack of control over what happens to them. Since those who maltreat them do so in a manner that is largely unconnected to the child's behaviour, the lack of predictability in the child's world has massive ramifications for the development of their character. In particular, the uncertainty as to when the child will be hit, rejected, sexually exploited or otherwise maltreated, allied to an inability to do anything about it, are the most damaging aspects that are common to all forms of child abuse: it leaves the child with no sense of control over his or her environment, and with a deep sense that other people are a potential source of harm and that the world they inhabit is an unpredictable and dangerous place. Adults who have been abused as children often speak not of the actual abuse being the worst part of it, but the helplessness and terror of anticipation, the *uncertainty*. It is for this reason that children often resort to desperate attempts to maximize the predictability of their world and the actions of others in it. Conditions of uncertainty and threat are the developmental experiences upon which fragile personalities are formed – the fearful and shaky foundations of character that will lead to so much chronic insecurity and often unshakeably low self-esteem.

The strategies that children adopt in desperate attempts to regain a semblance of control over their world, over their bodies, over their emotions and in relation to other people, are the foundations for so much that will sooner or later be viewed as 'abnormalities' or signs of a 'mental disorder'.[3] These strategies and the experiences out of which they arise will be the basis for those forms of distress that persist through adolescence and into adulthood: 'chronic' depression, anxiety, phobias, mood swings, obsessions, compulsions, psychosis, the various forms of self-harm (including the eating 'disorders' and substance misuse), continued relationship difficulties, as well as the so-called 'personality disorders'. Chronic forms of personal distress are the embodiment of prolonged exposure to conditions of uncertainty and threat. There are different ways that children can adapt to distress, and it is inevitable that some children will respond to these experiences by behaving in destructive ways. Herein lie the roots of so much that will be classified as delinquency in children, and badness or madness in adults.

All children adapt to and learn from their environment, and especially those around them, but children who experience the uncertainty and threat of abuse or neglect face particular difficulties when dealing with the extreme demands that their environment places upon them. It is perhaps important to distinguish here between the 'normal' fears and anxieties that children have, which are generally transient and not as severe or prolonged as the forms of distress that are caused by maltreatment. Much of what follows needs to be considered in this context. Those who are maltreated will always try to make their world more predictable and thereby to try and regain some control over what happens to them, even if that form of control is illusory or even self-defeating. Children become distressed in many of the same ways that adults do and as such they can become obviously anxious, fearful, withdrawn and depressed. They may experience nightmares or displace their fears of threat and uncertainty on to other objects or animals by developing intense phobias (for example, fear of spiders or a fear of the dark). They may attempt to regain a sense of control over what happens to their bodies, and the most obvious form this takes is by either refusing to eat or eating constantly or in huge amounts, or adopting either one of these strategies or the other at different times. Such strategies may develop into the so-called 'eating disorders' of anorexia nervosa, bulimia and obesity. The eating disorders develop directly out of a person's sense of powerlessness over their lives, and frequently this relates to sexual abuse in particular.

Maltreated children essentially have two strategies available to them. Either they try and take control in an *active* way by influencing their world, or they develop a very *passive* stance in relation to events or people around them. While some children do all they possibly can to avoid being maltreated, others will adapt their behaviour in ways that seem to actively increase the likelihood of further harm. This can be seen in some children who have been sexually abused when they behave in seemingly sexually precocious ways that are inappropriate for their level of development or, later on, putting themselves as teenagers in vulnerable sexual situations or being actively promiscuous. Similarly, in physical or emotional abuse children may behave in ways that are likely to lead to them being hit, shouted at or rejected. The key to understanding these strategies is that by behaving in these ways children give themselves a degree of control over *when* they are harmed: in this way a child can at least remove some of the uncertainty if not the threat. Also, some neglected children will often act in destructive ways simply because it is the only form of behaviour that receives a response from those around them. Even if the response they provoke is harmful to them, it feels better than being ignored: for some children, any form of social interaction is better than none.

There are a range of more 'passive' adaptations that children adopt in order to cope with their maltreatment. These strategies might involve children becoming very compliant, avoiding participation in social activities, or being unable to initiate any social contact. In its most extreme form, children can quite literally stop 'acting' at all. Children may learn that the only way to avoid being harmed is for them to become so passive that they are almost inactive. Victims often speak of this in terms of trying to make themselves 'invisible' so as to draw as little attention to themselves as possible. This adaptation is so often the origin of chronic depression, the form of distress that people experience when they are no longer able to act effectively. Experiments on animals have repeatedly shown that if you subject them to completely unpredictable harm (usually in the form of an electric shock) and that harm is applied in such a way so that it bears no relation to the animals' actions, they quickly learn to become almost totally inactive. Children can become withdrawn in just this way, accepting whatever happens to them with passivity and helplessness. I have seen many African children who have been reduced to this way of coping following periods of civil war and violent unrest in their countries.

Another passive adaptation is that children may learn to be hyper-vigilant and keenly attentive so as to try and anticipate the moods and behaviour patterns of the adults around them, anxiously watching out for the warning signs of danger. They may try very hard to ensure that they give their perpetrator no reason for attacking them by being very compliant and 'perfect' – even better than 'well behaved'. They can become fearful of witnessing conflict between others to the extent that they will always act so as to try to dissipate the situation.

Most forms of child maltreatment take place in private in hidden settings, out of public view. Since children cannot readily understand, let alone disclose, what is happening to them, their distress will inevitably manifest itself in a myriad of indirect ways, some more obvious than others, and some so obvious that it is remarkable that they are not noticed. No one draws attention to themselves without a reason. The dismissive phrase 'attention-seeking behaviour' is used to 'explain' someone's actions, but in fact explains nothing. It simply begs the question as to why someone is seeking attention and why in that particular way. What is it that the child is trying to draw attention to? Every form of human behaviour is also a form of communication – we do not act without meaning, even if we act without awareness of the meaning ourselves or if that meaning is obscure.

In general, children are far more likely to express their distress through their behaviour rather than through words. In young children this may manifest itself in chronic bedwetting or soiling, but more usually in their conduct in relation to other people. They may be very clingy or constantly behave in ways that draw attention to themselves or, conversely, withdraw and avoid their peers or other people. Very distressed children may self-harm in various ways; as well as attempting to kill themselves, they may hurt or cut parts of their bodies, or misuse drugs or alcohol. Some children will run away from home and live on the streets, becoming vulnerable to further abuse and exploitation. A significant majority of children who are driven into child prostitution have run away from violence at home. Persistently disruptive and unmanageable behaviour, so often seen as signs of illness, naughtiness or badness in children, is often the only way troubled children have for expressing their distress. This may take the form of unsettled or difficult behaviour either at home or at school: poor concentration, impulsivity, inattentiveness and general uncooperativeness.

They may also be aggressive towards other children or their teachers, or engage in bullying where they have an opportunity to be in control and to feel powerful over others. Children who bully rarely act in isolation, but typically recruit others around them to bolster their effectiveness and their power. Collective verbal and physical abuse relentlessly aimed at individual children from their peers can be a particularly vicious and destructive form of violence. Yet children's persistently aggressive behaviour is invariably an expression of their own experience of powerlessness and their need to be in control. Repeatedly studies have shown that children, even as young as age one, who are subjected to physical and emotional violence are many times more likely to be violent and aggressive than those who have not.[4] Children can *learn* that the most effective way of being in control is through the use of aggression and, furthermore, their aggressive behaviour can also be seen as an attempt to draw attention to their own experiences of violence elsewhere.

Sexual abuse and physical violence against children both involve pain, sometimes of an extreme nature, and there is one particular 'strategy' or adaptation that children (as well as adults in similar situations) use at the time in order to bear the experience. This adaptation is known as 'dissociation' or detachment, and is an effective way of coping with violence in situations where the victim is unable to fight back or to run away. The degree to which children 'anaesthetize' themselves in this way varies according to the form the violence takes as well as the degree of powerlessness experienced. Some adults who were repeatedly beaten as children describe themselves as having 'refused' to show their feelings to their abuser, either because to do so invited further ridicule or further violence, or because they did not want the abuser to have the satisfaction of knowing they had hurt them. At this level of defiance, in the absence of any other form of immediate resistance, the victim is in some way aware of what they are doing.

In sexual abuse, victims sometimes describe the experience as a more total process of depersonalization, where they no longer feel part of their bodies at all. They may imagine themselves to be somewhere else or experience the abuse as if it is happening to someone else while they are looking on. Of course, they do still feel the pain, sometimes to a greater extent once the perpetrator has stopped abusing them, and even for some time after the incident of abuse. Anyone who has experienced severe shock will have some personal understanding of this process of depersonalization. These self-protective processes that enable the child to cope with extreme situations of betrayal and violence by detaching themselves from their feelings can become part of who they are and how they operate and function in the world. Such children may learn to exist without emotional expression and without feeling and are seen as cold and detached. They may continue to be emotionally void in subsequent personal or intimate relationships, and this can also lead to adults being unable to feel anything towards their own children when they themselves become parents. When people become distantly detached from their emotions, this is often diagnosed as a symptom of 'schizophrenia' or of a 'personality disorder'.

One of the most disturbing forms of personal distress is what psychiatrists call 'schizophrenia' (or 'psychosis'). Although it literally means a 'split mind', this does not refer to a split into multiple personalities as is commonly supposed or that is so often portrayed in Hollywood films. It in fact refers to a split from 'reality' characterized by either delusions or hallucinations, or a split of the intellect from feelings and emotions. Since we are creatures of meaning and since language is such a vital aspect of our ability to relate to one another, it is this that makes schizophrenia the most disorientating form of distress and the one that most people associate with 'madness': psychosis is often characterized by an individual whose language and meaning no longer readily makes sense to other people. Despite the fact that the delusions and disturbances associated with psychosis are at times impossible to make sense of, it is still often a manifestation of personal distress like any other, differing only in form and content. There are many enduring 'mental' repercussions for those who were maltreated as children, which are often misinterpreted as being evidence for psychiatric abnormalities. For example, adults may suffer unwanted and persistent recollections of their abuse. This can be in the vivid form of a 'flashback', when the past and the present literally merge as the original experience of violence is relived as if it is actually happening all over again. They may experience a form of hallucination as they hear their abuser's voice, see their face or smell them. I have worked with many people whose 'voices' were the voices of their abuser tormenting them, echoes reverberating from the past. I once worked with a man diagnosed as schizophrenic, whose wealthy father used to drunkenly stand over him as a child and go on and on about what a useless, 'good for nothing' failure he was and how he would never amount to anything. Every time this man came close to achieving anything in his life he would be tormented by voices echoing his father's words and criticisms. He would then become gripped by an overwhelming sense that other people were judging him critically and mocking him to such an extent that he drank alcohol excessively to cope with this, became verbally aggressive, and then hid in his bedroom for days on end. Paranoia, or feelings of persecution, are typically viewed by professionals as delusional and illusory rather than in many cases as the justifiable anticipation of future harm based upon past experience.

Other forms of mental distress can emerge as delusions, seemingly fantastical belief systems or via the use of idiosyncratic and unintelligible language. Once again, such seemingly delusional ramblings are often the person's attempts to make sense of a confusing world. The form and content of the delusions are often not only significant, but also develop meaningfully out of that person's experiences, even if those experiences are unavailable for scrutiny.

The work of R. D. Laing and his colleagues demonstrated how the delusions and idiosyncratic beliefs that are supposed to characterize schizophrenia can make sense if they are placed back within the person's family processes and forms of communication, when the entire family is considered as a whole.[5] Laing and his colleagues focused on confusing forms of communication and what could be considered emotional abuse, but they did not consider the possible involvement of other forms of child abuse in the families they studied. More recent studies have also ignored the possible occurrence of concealed familial violence in the development of 'schizophrenia'. However, these studies have repeatedly shown that families at least contribute significantly to the emergence of subsequent 'psychotic episodes' or relapses,[6] even though the authors consistently stop short of accepting that the same families might have anything to do with the development and onset of the distress in the first place.[7] In particular, the concept of 'expressed emotion', in which relatives of those with schizophrenia are harshly critical of them, has found to be predictive of relapses as is spending too much time in direct contact with such relatives.

Powerlessness and dependency

Once a child has been abused, particularly if that abuse is sexual and persistent over time, the tremendous sense of powerlessness they experience in relation to the perpetrator is often hard for the public to understand, let alone those individuals who are (or were) locked into an abusive relationship.[8] Part of the passivity and compliance stems from the difference in power between the perpetrator and his victim: typically the perpetrator will be much bigger, older, much stronger physically, in a position of authority over the child, or a figure of public respect (for example, a priest, a tutor or a grandfather). In addition, the abusers may be acting in a more organized and collective manner so that the child is being assaulted by several adults at the same time, or one after the other while the others look on. Having something harmful done to them that they have no means of stopping or avoiding, can lead to a process of literal petrification. It is hard to describe the degree of terror that is involved in such powerlessness, which effectively renders any action other than passive and silent compliance impossible. To display any defiance or resistance in this situation is often futile, and may only make matters worse for the victim. To be in a situation and not to know how to act, and not to be able to respond, is tantamount to psychological and emotional annihilation. Victims describe this state of annihilation as being 'frozen' or as being in a trance, that they were unable to speak out, unable to scream, to run away or to fight back.

Perpetrators of persistent physical and sexual abuse (or domestic violence) can exert a degree of almost total control over their victims which often extends well beyond the abusive situation itself and can remain in place long after the abuse has stopped. Once the victim comes to feel helpless, worthless and yet at the same time responsible for the abuse, a distorted identification with the perpetrator, and an emotional dependency on them, often takes place. The victim's identity can become defined by their association with their abuser and they can remain compliant and passive in relation to them in situations that are unrelated to the abuse. This is the ultimate form of powerlessness, whereby the victim's entire sense of their own existence becomes dependent on the relationship with their abuser. This leads to an experience of being totally under the abuser's control and at the mercy of their every wish and command; it is as if the victim becomes 'spellbound'. Victims of sexual abuse in particular often do not understand why they were unable to do anything to stop or prevent repeated assaults on them, or why they 'kept going back for more', and perpetrators may use this dependency as justification that the child must like what they are doing to them.

In among the conflicting blend of emotions, some children will quickly grow to hate their abusers intensely, and if the abuse is sufficiently cruel and prolonged, a tiny minority of these children will fight back – and sometimes even kill the people abusing them. For most others, their hatred and rage may become so deeply embedded within them that it will sooner or later be directed towards themselves or other people. They may also feel angry towards, and betrayed by, other adults who may not have been involved in the abuse, but who failed to protect them or who brought the abuser into their lives. Though it might seem to make more sense for abused children to hate the actual person who assaulted them, within the arena of brutalized relationships the situation is far more complex than that. As well as a continued fear of the perpetrator and the entrenched position of passivity and powerlessness towards them, there may be other emotions that maintain the abuser's control over the victim. There may well be aspects of the relationship that are quite appropriate, or indeed even pleasurable and nurturing. Any scrap of kindness from a perpetrator becomes disproportionately significant to their victims who feel unworthy of it, no matter how small a part that kindness plays in their relationship. In sexual abuse, the illusion that they are loved or in some way 'special' to the perpetrator may also generate a tremendous sense of loyalty in some children towards their perpetrators and keeps them compliant and 'locked into' continual and repeated abuse. As well as being directly dependent on their abuser in other ways, say financially or through the perpetrator's status or authority, this sense of loyalty and emotional dependency may continue unchallenged well into adulthood. Frank Beck, for example, is estimated to have systematically abused some 200 children while he was in charge of three children's homes in Leicestershire. In 1991 he was given five life sentences as well as an additional twenty-four-years for abusing children who were placed under his care. He was said to have remarkable powers of control over these very difficult children and used perverse notions of 'regression therapy' not only to abuse them, but as justification to Social Services for his methods of 'treatment'. Yet a number of those who were abused by him remained in contact with him long after they left care, seeking his advice, and even inviting him to their weddings. The children of Fred and Rose West, despite years of systematic sexual torture and physical abuse by their parents, still speak of loving them and remaining loyal to them. The same experience of emotional dependency may also develop in other relationships in which violence is employed. Despite confusing and often ambivalent emotions, the creation of feelings of dependency, worthlessness and the imperative to please is often a significant part of the reason why women stay unshiftingly loyal to their violent partners.

Emotional abuse and cruelty can also lead to a dependency on the perpetrator where logically one might expect the victim to want to get away and avoid further harm. As we have already seen, children who are treated in this way can become clingy and try all the more to be close to or please the very person who is rejecting or criticizing them most. Even in later life, no matter how badly they may have been treated by the adult, the abused are often the first ones to defend or to help them. They may literally try for years to please their tormentor in a desperate and often futile attempt to gain their approval and acceptance, even though decades of adulthood experience indicates clearly that this will never happen. Almost without exception in my own clinical experience, it is the least favoured child in a family who is the one who lives nearest to and does most for their parents in their old age. Similarly, the fear of losing out on any inherited money and material benefits can also lead to children maintaining their compliance towards their controlling parents well into their own adulthood.

Self-blame and self-hatred

People who have been on the receiving end of all forms of violence, but especially if that violence takes place over a period of time, all too readily fall into the trap of self-blame, condemning themselves for what they should or should not have done. Particularly from a child's limited viewpoint, if they are being abused or hurt, then this must be because they are intrinsically bad, because of what they did, or because of what they didn't do or were unable to do. For a child there is no other explanation that makes sense. In addition, this notion is reinforced by those who harm them, as they often assert that what is being done to the child is the child's fault or for his or her own good. As we have seen, the belief that they themselves are responsible or to blame for the abuse is almost universally held by victims and they will carry this belief with them into adulthood. More than this, victims often feel deeply ashamed of what they have been through. The notion of badness becomes central to the child's view of himself or herself, so that anything bad that happens is in some way deserved. It is one of the principal reasons that victims stay so silent about their experiences, even for decades after the events, and this silence contributes in a substantial way to the collective belief that such experiences are uncommon.

This self-blame can readily turn into self-hatred or self-loathing, and the anger that might more legitimately be turned against the perpetrator – but that cannot be expressed through fear – is turned against the self and the body via the various forms of self-harm. All of the forms of self-harm also serve the purpose of distracting the person's attention from recollections of what has happened to them, or avoiding feelings that are associated with being abused, whether they are consciously aware that this is the case or not. Similarly, I have worked with many people who have taken an overdose of tablets not because they wanted to kill themselves, but because they could no longer bear the intensity of their distress. They may have felt unable to cope with intense feelings or disturbing recollections, or they may have been driven by the conviction that they were so bad that they deserved further punishment. For others, however, the ultimate control that they can have over their destiny is by attempting (or succeeding) to take their own lives.

Importantly, self-hatred is largely based on blame associated with having been a child who was maltreated. When these children become adults themselves these feelings can generalize to a hatred for all children, even – and especially – their own, since all children are seen as intrinscially bad or weak and therefore in need of punishment or deserving of harm. From such an unforgiving viewpoint, the innocence, vulnerability and dependency that is an integral part of childhood is seen as representing weakness, and therefore worthy only of hatred and contempt; often without any conscious awareness, normal childhood behaviour or displays of frailty and dependency can 'remind' people of their own experiences of childhood powerlessness. For some people such a reminder becomes unbearable, and for some children the consequences will be fatal.

Self-hatred, deeply felt rage and the crippling effects of powerlessness in the face of uncertainty and threat all combine to form a highly combustible mixture. This hatred can be turned inwards in the form of self-harm or it can be turned outwards against the world and other people. There is without doubt a huge difference between the sexes in terms of the ways in which men and women adapt to their experiences of abuse in childhood, with men and boys tending to *act upon their environment and other people* and women and girls tending to *feel and act upon themselves*. Despite decades of supposed equal opportunities, the women's movement and attempts to reshape Western cultural values towards the different sexes, there is still a vastly different emphasis in the gendered nature of child development. Masculine frameworks are still very much based on individual behaviour and control, whereas models of femininity tend to emphasize their collectivity, emotions and relative passivity. These profound differences in how children are brought up inevitably influence the ways in which girls and boys adapt to their maltreatment. Women far more readily turn their feelings of powerlessness, anger and hatred against themselves, whereas for men their need to be in control is turned against other people and their world.

With men, the expression of power through physical control and dominance may have to be fought for with relative equals, or much more readily acquired by attacking a target less powerful than the perpetrator. There is a generalized hierarchy from men attacking each other; men attacking women; adults attacking children; one child attacking another; and people harming animals. It is no coincidence that through the physical powers available to them, men can use their bodies to control, harm and abuse other men, but it is easier to harm women, children and animals. Men also use their sexuality as a form of violence to a far greater extent than women ever do. Women do not generally use their bodies in the same way as men: they are on the whole at least physically less powerful than men, and their violence and brutality is generally reserved for themselves or their children and is often expressed as emotional neglect or cruelty rather than in physical terms. As David Smail has pointed out in his insightful analysis of the relationship between power and distress, when men and women are stripped of all other forms of power so that they are reduced to the physicality of their bodies, men may resort to brute force and women to the bartering of their sexuality; that the relationship between a prostitute and her male pimp provides a revealing microcosm of the most basic forms of physical power available to people.[9]

The past and the future: from victim to perpetrator

The experience of powerlessness in violent or abusive relationships will of course shape in one way or another the kinds of relationships that are subsequently formed, either when the victims become adults themselves or when they move on to form other adult relationships. In both childhood and adulthood, there exists a range of stances: from almost total passivity in relationships at one extreme, to the other end of the continuum, where people actively seek various ways of being in control. It is also quite possible for the same person to be passive in certain settings and towards some people in their lives, and yet be extremely controlling in relation to others.

The most direct and immediate means of being in control in a relationship is, of course, through the use of violence, intimidation and aggression. Once violence has occurred in the context of a continuing relationship, then the mere threat of it is often sufficient to maintain the victim's compliance. Through their own use of aggression or violence a person can feel in control of situations and other people in which they were previously powerless: the cycle from victim to perpetrator is complete. It is also quite possible for the same person to be the victim of violence in one relationship and then to perpetrate violence on someone else, without there being any significant period of time (as, say, from childhood to adulthood) between the two. For example, women in violent relationships can be physically abusive to their children. There are of course other ways of being powerful and other means of controlling, harming and exploiting people without the need for employing violence. The possession of significant amounts of money or the attainment of positions of authority and status enable people to have control over their environment as well as the power to influence other people's behaviour. While it is possible for these forms of power to be used benignly and for the common good, the adage that power corrupts is as true today as it ever has been throughout human history.

The route between maltreated child to abusive or violent adult is a direct but meandering one, with many possibilities for diversion along the way. Many clients I see who have been abused fear that they themselves will abuse their own children because they have heard that there is such a link. However, *the majority of children who have been maltreated do not go on to become abusers.* Conversely, the fact that the overwhelming majority of maltreated children do not go on to become violent adults themselves is often seen as indicating that the link between the two does not exist or that it is at best a tenuous one. What is central to understand is the direction of the analysis of the link: that is, whether you look back in time *retrospectively* or forwards in time *prospectively*. For example, if you take 100 children who were physically abused and follow them into adulthood (prospectively), you find that only a small minority of them go on to become violent themselves – perhaps about ten of them. However, if you take 100 adults who physically abuse their children and you look back in time to their childhoods (retrospectively), you will find that the overwhelming majority will have been physically abused as children – about ninety of them. Put simply, while most people who have experienced maltreatment as children do not go on to become abusers or commit violent offences, the vast majority of adult abusers and violent offenders were themselves maltreated as children. The greater the severity and duration of harm that is inflicted on a child, the greater the likelihood of that child becoming violent. Emotional abuse, when taken in isolation from other forms of maltreatment, has to be especially brutal and prolonged for it to result in the child becoming a violent adult. If, however, you take another sample of 100 children who have been physically, sexually and emotionally abused, rejected and abandoned, and given no experience of genuine care, then the numbers who go on to become violent or abusers of children increases dramatically. Some maltreated children's violent behaviour (usually boys) can be traced without interruption from an early age right the way through their lives.

There are countless studies that accurately link adult aggression and violence to physical and emotional abuse in childhood. However, a significant proportion of adult violence, especially when that violence seems particularly sadistic, brutal or disturbing, is not related to these forms of abuse alone. If the blueprint in childhood for subsequent relationships is characterized by a confusing blend of powerlessness, fear, a detachment from emotions, dominance and control, then this may well lead to violence in adulthood. But if sexual abuse is also involved, then violence and brutality may become associated with intimacy and pleasure. It is within the arena of childhood powerlessness and brutalized intimacy that the origins of the most hideous and seemingly unfathomable acts of cruelty and violence are to be found. The act of rape for example, whether it be of teenagers or adult women and men, often may originate from the perpetrator's own experience of sexual abuse as a child or young person. These forms of interpersonal violence also typically happen to known victims in relationships, in private settings far away from public scrutiny, and, just as in the sexual abuse of children, the victims are rarely physically coerced into submission. More typically, the victim's total compliance is gained through intense fear, and victims often describe an overwhelming experience of powerlessness. Even in the case of 'stranger' rape, when the victim is not known to their assailant, many victims recount that the man who raped them would spend time talking to them, either before or after the attack, as if in intimacy.

With regard to the abduction and fatal sexual assaults on children that typically receive intense media focus, once again these forms of violence often have their foundations in the perpetrator's experience of childhood sexual abuse. Killing a child or an adult in these circumstances is about the assailant's attempt to have total control over their victim, an attempt to achieve their complete compliance and to ensure their permanent silence. In this distorted world where there is no distinction between pain and pleasure, some killers have even believed their fatal actions to be compassionate ones, simply because they could not bear to witness their victim's suffering.

There is ample evidence in the research literature that those who 'break the cycle' of abuse (from their own childhoods into their adult lives) have at some point been fortunate enough to form a meaningful, benign and supportive relationship with someone, and sometimes that other person has been a professional. In my experience, the most powerful antidote to the worst effects of child abuse is genuine and unconditional love. There are numerous people with whom I have worked who have been 'saved' by the presence of one loving relationship: the experience of being loved by somebody, however infrequent or distant, especially if that relationship is fairly constant over a period of time, can be the salvation of many young people and adults. However, professional forms of care are often no match for intrinsic love in its genuine form where there is no other motive or agenda involved. Being loved by someone who genuinely cares about you and who matters to you cannot readily be replaced by any statutory duty of care nor by any institution. In any case, as we shall see in Chapter 5, professional systems of 'care' have systematically failed to help the most vulnerable children, and have in many cases exploited and harmed them even further.

No one can escape an abusive childhood entirely unscathed,

and while most maltreated children do not become violent, a significant proportion of them will sooner or later enter the mental health system, or else struggle in one way or another with their health or in their personal relationships. However, it is important to reiterate that the vast majority of people experiencing personal distress are not, and will not become, violent themselves: violence and distress are opposite sides of the same coin. Though their roots are often the same, the reasons for differences between people in terms of the way in which their distress develops are often well beyond the powers of any individual to influence.

The most important single factor in the emergence of physical and especially sexual violence in later life is being male. As I have already discussed, the contribution of the obvious biological differences between men and women are often grossly exaggerated relative to the marked differences in the socialization of boys and girls. Beyond gender differences, the form a person's distress takes, and whether or not they become violent, is usually related to that person's 'fate' or the particular circumstances of their experience over the course of their lives. I have met a handful of people who have managed to hang on to their compassion against what seemed like overwhelming odds; in many ways it would be more interesting to find out how some people transcend their horrific backgrounds rather than study the ones who could not.

The age and sex of the victim, the severity and duration of their abuse and the presence or absence of mitigating experiences, will all combine to determine the nature of their response to their backgrounds. The occurrence of uncertainty and threat in childhood may or may not become a permanent feature of a person's personality. In either case, such early experiences will leave people extremely vulnerable when faced with situations of uncertainty or threat in later life. For some, the harmful events of their childhoods will be sufficient to make them violent regardless of what their adult circumstances are like. For most others, however, any distress or violent behaviour may only manifest itself later in their lives when they encounter further circumstances that are disturbing to them or beyond their control. This is essentially the difference between those who will be seen as being constitutionally 'mentally ill' or 'personality disordered' and those who are seen as only becoming so in relation to current life events.

Violent behaviour may be 'triggered' later in life by situations and experiences that pose a threat or that create uncertainty. Circumstances in which teenagers or adults feel powerless require a resonance with earlier experiences for the violence to manifest itself. When someone is said to have killed out of 'jealousy' or 'revenge', this needs to be understood in the context of profound insecurity and an extreme need to be in control. This then requires an explanation as to when such a degree of insecurity developed and how it becomes associated with control through violence. When intense jealousy or possessiveness become destructive, then this is often because of a deeply held mistrust of other people and relationships that may have nothing whatsoever to do with the current relationship, but instead be based on insecure relationships from the past. Similarly, alcohol, drugs, violent films, books and videos have all been blamed for violence, but each of these requires a personality that is *already* vulnerable to being violent for this to happen. People who are susceptible to confusing the imagery of videos and books with reality usually do so because for most of them their reality has in any case been far worse than anything they have watched or read.

Distress and personality

Those who grow up with prolonged experiences of uncertainty and threat that are an integral part of child abuse and neglect may have insecurity and fear permanently etched into their personalities; these experiences literally become physiologically and psychologically embedded. For some people, the experience of powerlessness in childhood and later in life may be all they have known. If they have had few benign experiences where they are given some degree of respect, self-determination and care, this becomes an integral part of their character, their psychology and their physiology; it is 'built in'. These are often the adults who were mistreated as children, or whose experience of childhood was chaos. Those who have little or no experience of being loved or cared about cannot develop any sense of themselves as being lovable, wanted, or worthwhile people or that they have any meaningful place in society. Respect for society and for other people or their rights simply cannot develop in the absence of having been treated with care. Almost regardless of what happens to them subsequently, such people will have a deep mistrust of others. The role models of relationships will be based on insecurity, impermanence and rejection as well as dominance and control. In addition to this, if they have also been sexually abused, then any form of intimacy will be inextricably linked to brutality. Many of these children will carry these models into all of the relationships they subsequently form. As such, many will be left with an inability to form or sustain meaningful relationships; and any that they do form will not be based on trust and respect, but will be characterized by insecurity and forms of control. They may respond to any potential threat of further rejection or separation with destructive actions. If they are women they are more than likely to find other relationships where they are further victimized or taken advantage of, either sexually, emotionally in the form of 'domestic violence' – or in all of these ways. In other words, they will be drawn towards a man or other relationships in which they will continue to be controlled. If they are men, then they are more likely to go on to form relationships with people in which they are the ones who are dominant and in control. It is quite common for relationships to be formed by two adults who both have the experience of abuse in their lives and who continue to victimize and be victimized by each other.

It is these people who will be left so poorly equipped to deal with life that they go on to make up the overwhelming majority of the long-term 'mentally ill' in psychiatric and forensic institutions.[10] Some will be so detached from their feelings as to be diagnosed as 'psychotic'. Others will be so disturbed and confused that they are barely able to communicate in any meaningful way with the rest of humanity. Unable to express themselves, the reasons for their distress will be literally lost in the mists of time. Some will become the men and women who try to control and cope with the intense feelings and thoughts associated with their past through the prolonged or heavy use of alcohol and drugs. Other people – since their past experiences of threat have become an integral part of who they are – will be seen as 'paranoid' because they attribute harmful intent to people and situations where there is 'objectively' none; some of them will inevitably become violent themselves – these are the people who will be seen and diagnosed as 'suffering' from an antisocial or 'psychopathic' personality disorder. Males in this group can be extremely and persistently dangerous as they possess no means of expressing themselves except through the use of coercion and violence. They move from one relationship to another, brutalizing and destroying the lives of virtually everyone they come into sustained contact with, subjecting the women (and sometimes children) in their lives to extremes of physical violence, vicious sexual assaults and sexual acts of degradation and subordination. They can come close to killing many people over the course of their lives, but often they know how to conceal their violence, how far to take their aggression, and just when to stop. Their victims do not report them. In many cases, these men are only caught and stopped when their actions prove fatal.

As we have seen in the previous chapter, the diagnostic categories of psychiatry have little or nothing to say about the development of the 'illnesses' they are supposed to define. In the absence of any meaningful acknowledgement of the sometimes terrible environmental conditions that shape people's personalities, such individuals and the ways in which they try to cope with their experiences will be defined as in some way or another 'abnormal'. In this way, people are all too often denied their history and pathologized for the ways in which they have developed and responded to their experience. The *Diagnostic and Statistical Manual of Mental Disorders* is one of the two major works of reference that attempts to classify and describe the myriad of psychiatric disorders.[11] Despite the inherent bias towards genetics and biological explanations within psychiatry, and ignoring the linguistic style of 'objectivity' with which the text is written, it is not at all difficult to imagine the kinds of malign or distorted experiences, particularly through childhood, that would give rise to the various forms of 'personality disorders', that it is supposed to describe. The *Manual* defines these in the following ways.

Paranoid Personality Disorder is a pattern of distrust and suspiciousness such that others' motives are interpreted as malevolent.

'Individuals with paranoid personality disorder are often difficult to get along with and often have problems with close relationships . . . . They are hypervigilant for potential threats . . . and appear to be "cold" and lacking in tender feelings' (p. 635).

'They are preoccupied with *unjustified* doubts about the loyalty or trustworthiness of friends or associates' (p. 637, my italics).

Schizoid Personality Disorder is a pattern of detachment from social relationships and a restricted range of emotional expression.

'They appear to lack a desire for intimacy, seem indifferent to opportunities to develop close relationships, and do not seem to derive much pleasure from being part of a family or other social group' (p. 638).

'Has little, if any, interest in having sexual experiences with another person. . . . Shows emotional coldness, detachment or flattened affectivity' (p. 641).

Antisocial Personality Disorder is a pattern of disregard for, and violation of, the rights of others.

Borderline Personality Disorder is a pattern of instability in interpersonal relationships, self-image, and affects, and marked impulsivity.

'Individuals with Borderline Personality Disorder make frantic efforts to avoid real or imagined abandonment' (p. 650).

Histrionic Personality Disorder

'Interaction with others is often characterized by inappropriate sexually seductive or provocative behaviour';
(p. 657).

'Is suggestible, i.e. easily influenced by others or circumstances . . . considers relationships to be more intimate than they actually are' (p. 658).

Avoidant Personality Disorder

'. . . A pervasive pattern of social inhibition, feelings of inadequacy . . . is unwilling to get involved with people unless certain of being liked . . . shows restraint within intimate relationships because of fear of being shamed or ridiculed . . . is preoccupied with being criticized or rejected in social situations. . . . Views self as socially inept, personally unappealing, or inferior to others' (p. 665).

Dependent Personality Disorder is a pattern of submissive and clinging behaviour related to an excessive need to be taken care of.

'. . . has difficulty expressing disagreement with others because of fear of loss of support or approval . . . urgently seeks another relationship as a source of care and support when a close relationship ends . . . is unrealistically preoccupied with fears of being left to take care of himself or herself' (pp. 668–9).

Similarly, the *ICD-10 Classification of Mental and Behavioural Disorders*[12] (the World Health Organization denomination of the diagnostic manual) defines personality disorders in the following way:

A specific personality disorder is severe disturbance in the characterological constitution and behaviour tendencies of the individual, usually involving several areas of the personality, and nearly always associated with considerable personal and social disruption. . . . They represent either extreme or significant deviation from the way the *average individual* in a given culture perceives, thinks, feels and, particularly, relates to others [my italics].

The *abnormal* behaviour pattern is enduring, or long standing ... the *abnormal* behaviour pattern is pervasive and clearly maladaptive to a broad range of personal and social situations ... the above manifestations always appear during childhood or adolescence and continue into adulthood [my italics].

For those who have some mediating experiences that allow them to develop a sense of their own humanity and self-respect, they may well channel their distress or their hatred and aggression into other areas that are more culturally acceptable. There are no limits to the variety of ways in which people deal with their traumatic or abusive backgrounds without initially or subsequently coming into contact with the mental health or criminal justice systems. There are many examples of extremely successful adults in all walks of life and in all professions who have had very damaging childhood experiences. Some may channel their aggression into military careers, and others will find acceptable expression for this in sports, the arts or business – obtaining great success in their chosen field. And some people who have abusive backgrounds make extremely sensitive and caring parents, who are tirelessly determined to avoid subjecting their own children to what they went through. However, even if they are successful in careers or as parents, most of those who have suffered abuse, trauma or neglect will suffer the consequences in terms of their low self-esteem and their inability to believe that they are worthwhile or lovable people. They will invariably have to struggle with their feelings of powerlessness and the inevitable effects that this will have on their health, their relationships and the ways in which they deal with further situations of uncertainty and threat throughout their lives.

That most people who have painful, traumatic or abusive experiences in childhood or later in life do *not* become violent is something that should be celebrated. It is a fact that for every person who responds to their experiences by becoming violent, there will be many more who do not. However, we should not be shocked surprised, or even mystified when some of us – when placed in circumstances which, for long enough, push us far beyond our limited resources to cope – adapt to those circumstances by resorting to destructive means of expressing ourselves.

·4·

Victims and Perpetrators

Mary

On 17 December 1968, eleven-year-old Mary Flora Bell from Newcastle was convicted of the manslaughter of two boys: Martin Brown, aged three, and Brian Howe, aged four. During the trial and in the weeks after it, the Press branded Mary a 'fiend', a 'monster' and a 'Svengali'. Though there was some acknowledgement of the terrible social and economic conditions that Mary grew up in, the reasons for her crime were largely seen as being due to her inherent 'evilness' – she was simply a bad seed. According to the Crown at the time of the trial, the murders were undertaken solely for the pleasure and excitement afforded by killing.[1]

The full extent of the abuse that Mary suffered before she killed the two boys did not surface for over thirty years until Mary agreed to collaborate on a new book about her life with the journalist Gitta Sereny, who had covered the original trial.[2] The account of some of what Mary endured as a child can be found in Chapter 1 under the heading 'Betty', who is the mother of Mary Bell – the 'Mary' referred to in that section. As in so many cases, there were loud and very clear warning signs of Mary's distress for many years preceding the killing of the two boys, all of which were misinterpreted as the bad behaviour of a naughty child. The more Mary attempted to draw attention to what was happening to her through her behaviour, the more misunderstood and dismissed she was. The less understood she was, the more extreme her form of communication became. Her acts of violence were the desperate attempts of a young child to show people the violence she herself was experiencing. Mary made repeated and very public attempts to implicate herself and her accomplice in the killings of the two boys. Indeed, she seems to have gone out of her way to do so, leaving notes for her teachers and others to find and even turning up at the children's funerals.

Mary's violence can be viewed not as the random and senseless acts of an evil or deranged child, but an *adaptation* to her own extreme experiences; in fact, her actions reflect exactly what she had herself experienced. Her mother soothed her, held her head, and spoke gently to her while the male 'customers' inflicted severe pain while abusing her, just as Mary reassured the boys while she strangled them. She laid her victims down and strangled them just as she had been laid down and held by the throat (or choked through oral sex). She scratched Brian Howe's legs with scissors just as the men had scratched her own legs as they abused her. Her detachment and emotional numbness, her 'cold staring eyes' – the very things that were repeatedly said in order to define her 'otherness' and her 'evil' – were features of her character that were a necessary and direct adaptation to years of rejection, emotional cruelty and sadistic sexual torture. More than this, the fact that she was arrested, charged and sentenced for the killings had the effect of removing her from a very abusive home situation. If drawing attention to herself was Mary's attempt to put an end to what was happening to her, then for a short while at least it had the desired effect.

To make *sense* of Mary's behaviour and personality requires an understanding of what had happened to her. Despite all her attempts to communicate the reasons for her distress, no one understood what her distress meant. Even though she broadcast her involvement in the children's deaths, no one took her communication seriously because no one wanted to believe a child could do such a thing; more to the point, no one could believe a child as young as Mary could inflict such violence because no one could believe that someone might have inflicted such violence on to her. Perhaps we can excuse this in the 1960s – after all, society at that time was naïve and ignorant about the nature and extent of child abuse; awareness of the signs of child abuse in a child's behaviour was not widespread; and systematic co-ordinated responses to child protection were barely developed. More recent events, though, illustrate how little we have learned from what Mary was desperately trying to tell us, and how ignorant we remain about these matters more than thirty years later.

Robert and Jon

The sheer volume of media interest in the abduction and killing of James Bulger and the manner of the coverage that the case received made it appear that this type of murder had never occurred before, let alone in this country. Though people naturally made links between the earlier case of Mary Bell, the sensationalized way the case was portrayed in the Press took this particular case to a different level and revealed much more about the nature of British culture in the 1990s than it ever did about the two young boys involved. As David Smith has shown, however, there is a hidden history in Britain of quite similar killings: 'similar cases have happened in Britain in recent times, in not so recent times, and long, long ago'.[3] In fact, since the Second World War there have been seventeen cases of children under the age of fourteen who have killed. Even as recently as 1988, a 'twelve-year-old boy abducted a two-year-old girl from a playground in Borehamwood and walked her just over a mile to a railway embankment, where he pushed her face into soft ground until she suffocated. The two had been seen by a total of seventeen people during the 40-minute walk following the abduction.'[4] While the circumstances of this murder are so hauntingly similar to the events surrounding the killing of James Bulger, this case received little or no national coverage and therefore did not generate nearly as much hype, hysteria or sensationalism. The names of the children involved have not been forcibly carved on to collective memory in a way that the names of James Bulger, Robert Thompson and Jon Venables have been.

Quite clearly, the killing of James Bulger proved to be the catalyst that unleashed all manner of opinions and vested interests, and became the focus for growing public concerns about the state of the nation. There have been few cases in history that have proved so valuable in terms of political expediency, with all the political parties pitching in their predictable interests. The Right's moralistic platitudes, coupled with their hypocritical emphasis on traditional family values, blamed the rise in the number of divorces, children born out of wedlock, and especially single mothers. We had the usual 'hang the bastards' mentality of the tabloid press linked with the Right's familiar law and order themes – more police, harsher sentences, more family discipline and, of course, the virtues extolled of a mythical Victorian era where children were dealt with harshly but fairly, and where they knew their place and respected their elders. The Criminal Justice Bill was gaining momentum at that time in Parliament, and this allied itself with a genuine sense of public outrage and soul searching about the nature of a society that could produce such young killers.

Once again, though, instead of answering the profound questions that this horrific crime raised about *society*, the nation settled into an all too familiar pattern of stressing individualism and impersonal rationality, and bringing about a collective distraction from the truth. Since the court case was merely there to prove whether Jon Venables and Robert Thompson had indeed killed James Bulger or not, and whether they 'knew' what they were doing was wrong, no one bothered to find out *why* they had done it. British High Courts are not interested in the reasons why such a brutal act manifested itself in two young boys; only the 'facts' of the case can be presented and, because of this, justice was not done. Justice was not done because on the basis of the evidence presented in court there was no *reason* for the boys to have committed such a vicious killing; no one attempted to make *sense* of their brutal actions. Instead, most people – not only in this country, but all over the world where the case generated huge interest – comforted themselves in the knowledge that these two boys were essentially an anomaly, an enigma; they were different from other boys, freaks. Even many of the 'moral majority' who were outraged at the violence that had occurred were themselves quite willing to physically abuse (or perhaps even kill) the boys as they were taken to and from court for their trial. Such people gathered outside the courts, and hurled abuse and threw bricks at the passing police vans containing the two little boys who found themselves at the epicentre of a massive social and political storm.

Lord Denning, in *The Sun* on 25 November 1993, was quoted as saying that the killing should be viewed as a 'freak incident for such terrible wickedness to come out in two lads'. After the trial, detectives involved in the case said that the two boys were evil and fixated on killing. Sergeant Phil Roberts said, 'These two were freaks who just found each other. You should not compare these two with other boys – they were evil. The other kick was fooling the public and the police.'[5] Mr Justice Morland described the abduction and murder of James Bulger as a cunning and wicked act of 'unparalleled evil and barbarity'. He then went on to say: 'It is not for me to pass judgement on their upbringing but I suspect exposure to violent video films may in part be an explanation.'[6]

There were wider social and political forces that all came together at that precise moment. Elizabeth Newson, a Professor of Child Psychology, had recently reviewed the evidence about the effects on children of violence on television and this had received much publicity.[7] Apart from the fact that there was little resemblance between the killing and a scene in the film *Child's Play 3*, which the children had allegedly watched on video, and although there was in fact scant evidence that the boys had watched this video, the major issue that was focused on, and even debated in the House of Commons, was the link between violent videos and the children's brutal behaviour. Once again, the collective capacity for distraction from the more direct and immediate material influences on the children was very clearly demonstrated. It is remarkable that a society should be extremely interested in the effects of violence on children from a television set, but barely interested in the effects of real-life violence on those same children.

During the trial itself, both prosecution and defence counsels colluded in the avoidance of evidence about the boys' family backgrounds, apparently so as to minimize their own families' suffering, as well as being a consequence of the use of the adversarial system adopted in such trials. Due to this seemingly compassionate legal gesture, no information about the children's background was offered as defence nor mitigation, and important crucial information was thereby systematically suppressed and withheld from the public debates that surrounded the trial and subsequent convictions. Astonishingly, the only defence that was offered was a reminder from Brian Walsh QC acting for Jon Venables, that the boy had shown remorse as he confessed to killing James: 'What about his mum? Tell her I am sorry,' he had said. Once again, an unusual but by no means unprecedented act of murder was pushed further and further into the realms of inexplicability.

It is worth noting that although they showed signs of severe emotional disturbance, they had 'no abnormality of mind'.[8] The report on Robert Thompson said that he showed 'no signs of any formal mental illness such as psychosis or a major depressive disorder'.[9] Since they were deemed to be of sound mind, the trial centred on the purely *rationalist* question, upon which the fate of these two boys was ultimately decided. If they were of sound mind and if they had planned their actions, they would be convicted of murder and be sentenced to life imprisonment. If they were seen to be the confused, poorly socialized and abused and neglected little boys that they were, then they would be guilty of manslaughter and no mandatory life sentence could be given. The central question from a legal standpoint appeared so simple: did they know right from wrong? If they did and they had planned the abduction and the killing, then in the eyes of the law and the rest of society they were 'cold blooded' murderers. According to the British criminal justice system, these boys did know the difference between right and wrong, and they had indeed planned the abduction and killing of a toddler. Experts who examined the boys to determine this were not asked to qualify their assessments with reference to the boys' own experiences. Neither *emotionally* based nor *developmental* psychological evidence was heard. Paul Britton, consultant forensic psychologist who had advised the police during their investigation, offered his own essentially rational explanation: 'they decided to kill him', 'it was a deliberate decision'; in other words, they rationally *chose* to do what they did.[10] The boys were branded 'evil', and then tried, convicted and sentenced as if they were adults. Simply because the adult world focused on their poorly formed rationality, the terrible mess that these children's emotional worlds were in was considered irrelevant. They may well have been sound of mind, but their hearts were in complete turmoil.

In its systematic suppression of information about the children's backgrounds the legal system also failed to hear vital evidence. By focusing almost exclusively on these two boys, the same process distracted attention away from whatever it was that had happened to them. In the eight months that it took for the case to come to trial, the boys were denied any form of psychological treatment for fear of 'contaminating' their evidence should it come to court. In as much as they were allowed access to psychiatrists or psychologists, they were only there to assess their capacity to tell right from wrong and whether they were 'mentally responsible' for their acts at the time of their crime. This seems all the more appalling and unjust when we consider the children's actual experiences, their home lives, their upbringings and their family backgrounds.

The children grew up in Walton. While perhaps not being the worst area in Liverpool, Walton remains a deprived, rundown, inner-city urban priority area. At the time of the killings, unemployment levels were more than twice the national average: '20 per cent, rising to nearly 30 per cent, among men and young people'.[11] For many families this was the third generation to be unemployed. While Jon's father had been unemployed for over a decade, Robert's was completely absent and had provided no financial support for his family, let alone had any contact with them for years. Both families lived in poverty.

Both children had a vast array of emotional and behavioural disturbances: truancy, shoplifting and theft, concentration and attention difficulties; both were disruptive and difficult to control in class, as well as educationally delayed. Both were prone to massive extremes in mood and behaviour, from being outwardly aggressive to being withdrawn and thumb-sucking – classic distress signals, signs that something was seriously amiss in the lives of both these children. Both spent substantial amounts of their time unsupervised, unmonitored and left to their own devices.

Robert Thompson was a child of chaos. His family lived on, near or under the notional poverty 'breadline'. They were shunned by their community, outcast, the butt of local criticism. If there were any criminal activities or troubles, the Thompsons were frequently blamed, and hence they were well known to the police. Robert was the fifth child out of seven. At the age of ten he was barely literate. Robert's father was violent and frequently drunk. He left his family for another woman five years before the murder took place. He left his wife to bring up his six children on her own with no financial support, and the family had no contact with him at all. The week after he walked out, the family's home burned down in a fire. They were eventually rehoused close to the railway yard where the terrible crime would take place several years later. Ann Thompson, Robert's mother, was also prone to heavy drinking and she was known to leave her children alone sitting outside their house for hours while she was in the pub. During the months after her husband walked out on her, she admits to having been drunk almost permanently, taking bottles of spirit to bed with her and drinking from them as soon as she woke up. At that time, her boys began to get in trouble with the police and social services became involved. She admitted that 'she had never been able to manage her life or give her children what they needed' and had herself taken an overdose in the years since her husband left her.[12] The two boys who had gone into care had also taken overdoses of paracetamol. On one occasion one of her boys was sent back from school for not having any shoes. He had outgrown his existing pair and she simply could not afford to buy him a new pair without help from a voluntary support group for families in need.

With his father gone and his mother struggling to cope, Robert was frequently left to wander the streets on his own, where he learned to be streetwise, hardened, stealing from shops, vandalizing. There was sequential bullying and violence among all the children in the family, with Robert's bullying having started by the time he was five. Each of the boys was said to be frightened of the next, and it has been reported that each of them assaulted and tied their younger brothers up. Two of the older boys had been in voluntary care since 1992, and some of the children were well known to the police. The oldest boy (nine years Robert's senior), who had been unable to find work by the time he was twenty, was described by his mother as having taken on the father's role for many years. Robert's upbringing was bewilderingly inconsistent – either he was experiencing severe emotional neglect, or 'getting shouted at and battered', or being treated 'like a soft, cuddly baby'. David Smith describes him at home as 'always sucking his thumb . . . he'd sit on his mum's lap and suck his thumb'.[13] As early as September 1989, teachers at Robert's school made several attempts to alert social services about the problems in the Thompson household and the sequential bullying between the boys. Despite this and the fact that he had been truanting regularly and consistently for several months before the crime, it was not until eight days before James's abduction that a meeting with Mrs Thompson was arranged.

Ann Thompson reported that she had always been frightened of her own father who had beaten her regularly and systematically with a belt. Her mother had not protected her from the ordeal of having to stand there and be beaten: she too was the victim of this man's violence, especially when he was drunk, and this was also done in front of the children. She said that she had always been unhappy and that she had wet her bed until she was fifteen. Her father's response to her bed-wetting was to beat her for it all the more. Unsurprisingly, she ran away from home at sixteen.

Jon Venables's family were not quite as poor as Robert's. There were only three children, with Jon being the middle one. His early life was characterized by domestic conflict and his parents separated when he was five. Jon's father had not worked since he was thirty; he lost his job in 1983. Jon's older brother, by three years, was born with a cleft lip and required a great deal of hospitalization. His mother described this older boy as a terribly unhappy and frustrated child, and that until he was four he was unable to express himself or talk. As a result of this, he spent a great deal of time crying and driving her 'berserk'. The youngest child, who was born a little over a year after Jon in 1983, also had mild learning difficulties and subsequently required special educational provision. All this was going on in Jon's first years of life, which suggests that he must have spent those first years in an atmosphere of extreme emotional tension. Susan Venables described feeling overwhelmingly trapped at that time, as if she were a 'prisoner in her home', and her husband's attitude was that all the pressures at home were her job – after all, he went out to work all day and didn't want to hear about how awful her day had been. He told her to 'get on with it'.

In 1983, when Jon was barely a year old, Susan's father died of cancer leaving her mother on her own. At the same time, Susan's husband lost his job; their relationship became acrimonious and they rowed a lot. They sold the house, and Susan went to live at her mother's while her husband moved to a bedsit. Despite living separately their relationship continued, albeit somewhat haphazardly. However, in a totally confusing set-up, Jon's parents continued to share each other's homes as well as the child-rearing – the children went to and fro with the parents from home to home and they all went on holiday together. There were times when Jon was living with his mother and times when he lived with his father.

By 1989 the oldest son was receiving respite fostering care as he was giving his mother problems on account of his temper outbursts. Throughout this period and up to the events of 1993, Susan Venables herself had a great number of 'medical problems'. By the time Jon was seven, it was already apparent that he was both very unhappy and extremely disruptive at home and at school.

By 1990 his behaviour at school deteriorated markedly and he fell behind educationally. He complained about being regularly bullied. He was prone to outbursts of sudden anger and extreme violence at school, and he became extremely disobedient and alarmingly disruptive, rocking backwards and forwards and moaning strange sounds. If reprimanded, he was known to bang his head against the wall and fall on to the ground and throw his arms around. At other times he banged his head against furniture and cut himself and his clothes with scissors, or pulled objects and displays off the classroom wall. He regularly began to throw objects at other children. Eventually he was suspended for two days after holding a ruler to another boy's throat and having to be forcibly pulled away. Despite having been to the school on a regular basis over this period, Susan Venables later claimed that she knew nothing of Jon's problems at school. She kept her son away from school for ten weeks following the suspension, and said that she had taught him herself over that period.

Jon started truanting when he met Robert at a new school in September 1992. They had both been dropped down a year due to their poor academic progress. When asked why he had become friends with Robert, Jon said that he felt sorry for him because his mother didn't care about him. During the school term preceding the crime on 12 February 1993, Robert missed thirty-seven half-days, and Jon missed four half-days, out of a total of sixty. Those four occasions that Jon truanted coincided with dates that Robert was also absent from school.

The fact that the children displayed such severe behavioural and emotional disturbance is, with little doubt, the direct consequence of their own abusive experiences, ranging from complete neglect, erratic and chaotic developmental boundaries, complete emotional confusion as well as cruelty, and through to bullying and physical violence. If that were not enough, further clues as to what these two boys had themselves experienced are revealed by the actual manner of the prolonged and violent attack on James Bulger on that horrific 2½-mile journey. Bricks, stones, paint and a piece of metal appear to have been thrown at James, and he was kicked in the face and body. He sustained many fractures to the skull, and death resulted from multiple blunt-force injuries to the head. He was already dead by the time an oncoming train had severed his body into two after it had been left on the railway track, apparently in a pathetic attempt to make his death look like an accident.

Once again, from an explanatory point of view, vital features of the attack received virtually no media coverage either at the time of the trial or in the coverage following it; namely, that there was an unmistakable *sexual* element in the killing. At some stage on that fateful journey, James's shoes, socks, trousers and underpants had been removed and, having been undressed, his penis and foreskin had been manipulated. There was some evidence that nearby batteries had been inserted into James's anus. There were terrible injuries to his mouth – eventually Jon Venables told his father that they 'had pushed batteries into the baby's mouth'.[14] Both Jon and Robert displayed their most extreme distress, anxiety and very obvious discomfort when asked about any of the sexual features of the attack during the initial police interviews. When asked about some dirt that had been noticed on the evening of the killing, Robert asked his interviewer to clarify what he meant by 'dirty marks':

Interviewer: 'You know what dirty marks are, don't you?'
Robert: 'Like sex marks.'
Interviewer: 'Like what?'
Robert: 'Sex marks. Dirty.'[15]

Much of the sexual attack, as well as the infliction of pain that was intimately bound up in the whole process, took place in the darkness and in a private, hidden and secluded but familiar place to which James had been systematically led for over 2 miles. It is quite possible therefore that the boys had not intended specifically to kill James, but that they had 'intended', consciously or not, to commit a brutal sexual attack with all the features associated with the way in which many children are sexually abused by adults. The specifically and unmistakably sexualized nature of the killing is not a random feature, neither is the way in which they took him to a secret and private location to do so. Added to this was the two boys' extreme distress over any questioning about the sexual element to the attack. All of this strongly suggests that in addition to physical abuse and neglect, at least one of the boys was sexually abused as well.

Fred and Rose

The events at 25 Cromwell Street in Gloucester involving Fred and Rose West, the twenty years of horrific murders and sexual torture, have now become well established in the annals of British crime. At the very heart and soul of all the crimes that the Wests committed was the violence and betrayal and confusion that is sexual abuse. Virtually all of their crimes displayed a confusion between dominance, control and brutal intimacy which are all too familiar features of this form of violence against children. Fred and Rose took it one step further and into the realms of total control that is murder. The very last moments of each of their victims's lives was characterized by them being subjected to physical and sexual assaults while being completely and utterly powerless to do anything about it: they were mostly bound and gagged before they were slowly tortured to death. Even in the manner of the disposal of the bodies, Fred West still maintained control over them by keeping them near him and buried in his house. The fact that the Wests' actions are the far end of the continuum, the extremity that confuses control with death, does not disconnect it from the rest of child abuse and from other forms of violence as well. Their actions differ only by degree and not by nature. As a measure of the degree of control that Fred and Rose exerted over their victims, Rose's brother Graham reported that when he visited his sister at her home in Cromwell Street, the children were cowered and came across as timid. They required only the merest glance from their mother to stop whatever they were doing if she felt they were misbehaving. Part of Fred's own personalized form of tyranny was that he had microphones in every room so that he could potentially monitor any conversation that occurred as well as listen in to any sexual activities.

It should not by now come as any surprise to discover that both Fred and Rose had very abusive and destructive backgrounds. Rose's childhood was characterized by sexual abuse, teenage rape, loneliness, abandonment and emotional neglect. According to her brothers, Rose's father – who died in 1979 – was extremely violent to her mother and all of the children, taking a knife to them and grabbing their hair and smashing their faces against a wall. We know her father sexually abused both her and, eventually, his step-granddaughter, Anne-Marie.

Rose met Fred when she was only fifteen, and her mother has said that she didn't take to Fred, that she thought he was a liar and deceitful. In a remarkably drastic attempt to end the relationship between Fred and her daughter, Rose was put into care by her mother in 1969 and was described as 'uncontrollable'. Given that we now know that she had already been sexually abused by her father, her behaviour might well have been 'out of control'. More than this, however, Rose's physical and sexual abuse by her father meant that she would have been particularly vulnerable to an older man with a powerful and controlling personality. As I have pointed out in Chapter 3, the continual and repeated retraumatization of an adult who has been abused as a child is very common. Like moths drawn to candles, the abuse leaves them extremely vulnerable to further destructive and harmful relationships. Indeed, several newspapers when commenting on Rose's initial relationship with Fred seemed to forget that she was a child herself when she met him, and only portrayed *her* as sexually predatory or rampant. They also seemed to forget that when they met, Fred was eight years her senior, had a history of violence, and had already killed at least one person. That Fred was having under-age sex with Rose seems also to have been overlooked: she was already pregnant with Heather by the time she was sixteen. In this sense, Rose, regardless of whether she went on to collude with and participate in her husband's distorted and violent world, was as much one of Fred West's victims as were all the other women he tortured and killed. Of the estimated 5 percent of child sexual abuse that is carried out by women, a significant majority of this occurs in conjunction with a man who is often coercive and controlling in the relationship with his female accomplice, and often abusing her as well. A journalist covering the trial commented that Rose presented herself in a strikingly similar way to her surviving victims.[16] However, Fred's brother Doug West said after the trial that 'I would put most of the blame on Rose', a sentiment that seems to have been widely held.

Fred West was born in 1941 in Much Marcle in Herefordshire. He was barely literate and it is clear that he also came from a family where there was a high degree of violence and sexual abuse. Both his parents were said to be involved in the abuse, sexual or otherwise, of all six of their children. It is said that Fred was sexually abused by his mother at the age of twelve. We also know that Fred was expected to kill animals on the family farm from a young age. At the age of eighteen Fred was involved in a motorcycle accident and spent eight hours lying unconscious in a ditch before he was found. Relatives say he was never the same after this. If he did receive a serious head injury at this time, it is quite possible for this to lead to a disturbing lack of inhibition in his behaviour and speech, common in many head trauma patients. If this was the case, then it hardly supports the view that Fred was born innately evil. After their mother's trial was over, several of their children commented that Fred could not always remember their names. In any case, throughout his life Fred displayed all of the inappropriate speech and behaviour associated with a traumatized sexuality following childhood sexual abuse, all of which would have been far worse if he had 'neurologically' lost his inhibition as well. He made no secret of his obsession with sex and regularly made inappropriate suggestions and passes at women. His statements to police clearly show his immature preoccupation with sex and his obsessively sexualized distortion of other people's behaviour. He often talked about sex and women in inappropriate ways, insisting that they were all prostitutes who only wanted one thing. Fred believed that his daughters should be 'broken in' sexually by their father and he became violent if they showed any signs of refusing him. He would order his daughters to walk in front of him naked and would tell them that 'boys don't do it properly, dads know how to do it right'.

He told police during interviews that all young women were only interested in sex and his victims had forced themselves on him because they were 'so desperate for it'. He made no secret of the sexual activity at his home, telling his work colleagues of sex parties they were holding in the evening. He even boasted to colleagues that he had carried out many abortions on women. All of his children reported that he had a vicious and violent temper.

The case of Fred and Rose West and the countless young women that they tortured and killed over a period of decades reveals as much about society and its attitudes to violence and child abuse over this period of history as it does about them as an extreme married couple. It is so much easier to see them as freaks that are fundamentally different to everyone else. As Detective Superintendent John Bennett, who led the investigation, put it on the day of Rose's conviction: 'It is clear that Mrs West must be a psychopath. She and Fred were a perfect pair for each other.'[17]

Accumulated over thirty years were files held by police, the courts, schools, and education, social services, the NSPCC, family doctors and hospitals all involving various members of the West family and their victims. There were quite literally hundreds of people in contact with the West family and the house at Cromwell Street: the hundreds of 'customers' who took part in the prostitution offered by Rose and the sexual prostitution of the children at the house; the neighbours; the countless lodgers who stayed and the fortunate ones who left; the family's relatives. There were numerous contacts with many different agencies, all of whom failed to perceive the extent of what was happening, failed to make adequate sense of the catalogue of signs they were given. The Bridge Child Care Consultancy Service was commissioned by Gloucestershire's County Council to investigate the role of statutory services and the years of contact that they had had with the West family. Their investigation fell far short of the full public inquiry that the case merited. The Bridge report was critical of the many agencies involved, though it essentially exonerated them of any major responsibility for events at 25 Cromwell Street. As well as highlighting lapses within the police, the health and education bodies, the social services and the NSPCC, the investigation revealed that part of the failures were due to a lack of communication within and between agencies. They concluded that the warning signs were missed because of a general cultural view that, at that time, did not accept that widespread sexual abuse existed within the family. The report's main conclusion was that on the basis of the information available, no one could have predicted that the family was at the centre of multiple murders. Indeed, it would not be fair to expect anyone to have realized from these contacts that countless people had been killed, but the evidence of child abuse *was* overwhelmingly clear. There was a catalogue of failures in child protection that could have easily led to the discovery of the full extent of the less visible violence.

Michael Honey, chief executive of Gloucestershire County Council, warned against judging events with the benefit of hindsight: 'Care agencies are now much more vigilant and better trained. They work together better and their systems have been tightened up. Warning bells would be heard today.'[18]

The NSPCC had had contact with the family four times in 1989 following a reported assault, but took no action after the complaint was withdrawn. On the day of Rose West's conviction, Jim Harding, the NSPCC chief executive, said: 'On the evidence before it at the time, which is very different to that available now, the NSPCC did not believe the case serious.'[19]

Jeff James, chief executive of the Gloucestershire health authority, said the NHS had had contacts with the family over thirty years, but nothing untoward had been spotted. He said that we should resist seeking scapegoats among health bodies and Social Services: 'It would have required remarkable perception and abilities to penetrate the web of deceit spun by Frederick and Rosemary West.'[20]

In reality, there was no web of deceit. The fact that the systematic abuse of children and young people went on for over thirty years had nothing whatsoever to do with the powers of deception that Fred and Rose West supposedly possessed. The sexualized world of abuse and control and violence that Fred and Rose created around themselves was literally littered with signs of what was going on. This was not a case of a cunning and devious couple who were so clever that they managed to conceal their hideous crimes from the world: the fact that they were able to do so *despite* the transparency of their abuse and other crimes involves us all. The fact that these warning signs were not picked up and acted upon reflects badly on a society that is not prepared to see the evidence before its eyes or to imagine that such abuse occurs, in varying degrees, all over the country all of the time.

As early as 1961 Fred was arrested for allegedly committing incest, but was released after evidence was withdrawn. He was already a violent young man in other ways in the early 1960s (when he would have been in his early twenties), as he was known to beat his first wife, Rena Costello, whom he had married in 1962. Indeed, the beatings eventually became so bad that Rena was taken away by some friends. As we now know, she was later to be one of his first murder victims.

Fred had often boasted to colleagues that he had performed abortions on women. In fact, in 1962 he had carried out an attempted abortion on his wife Rena which was reported to the authorities, but no action was taken.

Fred put his daughters Charmaine and Anne-Marie into care on five occasions between 1965 and 1970, and yet when Charmaine disappeared some time after 1970 no action was taken. At the end of 1970, Fred was jailed for ten months for minor offences of dishonesty, leaving the seventeen-year-old Rose entirely on her own to look after Charmaine and Anne-Marie (aged seven and five respectively) and her newly born daughter, Heather. The fact that Rose had only recently left the care system herself, but was looking after three young children on her own, does not seem to have been cause for concern. She wrote to Fred in prison and in one letter signed off 'Your ever worshipping wife, Rose'. She also wrote about mistreating Charmaine and how she hated her. Shirley Giles gave evidence at Rose's trial. She had lived in the top flat above Rose and the three young children at that time. Her daughter Tracey was sent down to borrow some milk and saw Charmaine tied to a chair with a leather belt.

In 1972 Caroline Owens was picked up by Fred and Rose while hitchhiking, and they offered her a job as a nanny. Feeling uncomfortable about Rose's increasingly sexual behaviour towards her, Caroline handed in her notice. On 6 December 1972, the Wests were driving by, saw Caroline, and offered her a lift. She was overpowered, bound and gagged and taken back to Cromwell Street, where she was violently assaulted by Rose and raped by Fred. He threatened to keep her in the cellar, use her as a prostitute for their black clients, and then to kill her and bury her body under the paving stones of Gloucester. She managed to escape the following day and eventually told the police. In January 1973 Fred and Rose admitted indecent assault at Gloucester Magistrates Court and were each fined £50. Caroline Owens said that she did not pursue a charge of rape against Fred West at that time because police warned her she would be subjected to a harsh cross-examination: 'one detective treated me badly and that put me off going to court'.[21] After the attack she suffered from severe 'depression' and terrible feelings of worthlessness. Four years after the assault, she took an overdose and had to be hospitalized.

Miss A, a key witness in the murder trial, did not report the violent assault against her in 1976: 'You couldn't go to the police then. There was a stigma. If you were in care you were bad.'[22] She both witnessed and was subjected to a violent assault by the Wests. She also tried to kill herself in 1983. In 1989 she was admitted to hospital suffering from 'depression' and had also taken refuge from a violent first husband. She also experienced flashbacks and waking terrors in which Fred appeared as a man in black. In 1990 she took another overdose.

Astonishingly, various members of the West family had thirty-one treatments at Accident and Emergency, as well as countless other hospital admissions between 1972 and 1992. These included many serious injuries for which different and unconvincing explanations were given. Several members of the family were treated for thrush, and one of the children even had gonorrhoea while still a minor. Fred was also treated for this disease at about the same time. In 1973 one of Fred's daughters, Anne-Marie, collapsed on her ninth birthday and was kept overnight in hospital. She was seen at Gloucester Royal Hospital and, though scratches and bruises around her breasts were noted, Rose West's explanations were accepted and no follow-up was carried out. On another occasion one of the daughters presented at the same hospital casualty department with vaginal injuries and, once again, Rose's explanation that the child had sustained the injury riding a bicycle was accepted at face value. Anne-Marie told of a teacher who had spotted her injuries when she was young and on one occasion an educational welfare officer had called round to the house at Cromwell Street. No follow-up was arranged and, as a result of the visit, Anne-Marie was given a vicious beating by Rose for having told her teachers. Anne-Marie was absent from school sixty times in her penultimate year, and yet no one investigated why. Though her mood swings and other forms of behavioural disturbance were recorded in her reports, again there was no follow-up. In 1980 this same child was admitted for the termination of a pregnancy. The child was her father's. She said that she was not even told she was pregnant and was not interviewed separately at any time. Once again, no checks were made with social services or the police.

In 1987 Fred told a teacher that he had 'laid Stephen out'. The teacher involved did not feel it merited a Child Protection Report. In 1988 an anonymous call to social services told of how the children were being left unattended and that Rose was working as a prostitute. No apparent cause for further investigation was found by the social worker who visited the house. In March 1989 a teacher telephoned the NSPCC and raised concerns about one of the children. Social services were informed, and though the child was seen for four months none of the horrors of his upbringing came to light. He indicated that he did not wish to be seen any more and contact was stopped. We are told that the NSPCC file was destroyed accidentally.

Throughout this time, the Wests had a stream of young lodgers in the top-floor bedsit at Cromwell Street, some of whom were sexually abused as well: young men and women, including Gillian Britt, who heard Rose's sexual activities and thought nothing of it until what she heard became so violent that she left. Journalists covering the case who were allowed into 25 Cromwell Street commented on how tiny the house was and how the rooms were so small that it would surely have been impossible not to hear what was going on from one room to another. There was a constant stream of 'customers' coming to the house for prostitution and sexual offences against the children, all of whom contributed to Fred's and Rose's sense that what they were doing was normal and acceptable.

In 1992 Fred was accused of rape on a minor, but several months later the case was dropped because the victim refused to testify. Some of the children were taken into care at that time, although some ran back home. When the evidence was withdrawn, the family hugged in court and Fred was released from the hostel where he had been sent.

When he worked at a home for people with learning disabilities, he told workmates that the women there were nymphomaniacs who asked him to sleep with them. Complaints about his behaviour reached management and he was asked to leave.

Over more recent years, he made constant remarks to his workmates about the prostitution that occurred at his home in Cromwell Street. He also made remarks to them about his own daughter, Anne-Marie, when she was helping him at work, telling them that 'her boobs are bigger than a handful now'. No one felt that such comments were cause for concern.

It is clearly evident that the Wests' children were moving in and out of the care system, and had a mother and father who had known criminal records and histories of sexual offences against young people. Many of the children displayed the well-documented signs of distress associated with child abuse in their behaviour at school, with sufficient levels of disturbance to have caused concern for their teachers. Some of the children ran away from home and sought help from various agencies; others disappeared altogether. Prosecutions of child sex abuse cases against Fred were brought and then dropped at the last minute. Were the witnesses supported adequately? Were they intimidated out of giving evidence? Immediately after the case, the local police force issued a public denial of the suggestion that any of its staff had visited the Wests' home – that is, in an *unofficial* capacity. So were there influential public officials who availed themselves of the services that were on offer at the house? This was not Britain in some pre-war era of ignorance and innocence on matters of child abuse. This was Britain in the 1990s, after several inquiries had already repeatedly highlighted the need for various agencies to work together to protect children. Police, doctors, nurses, teachers and social workers were already supposed to be working closely together to collate information about children at risk of abuse. The fact that Fred's and Rose's thinly veiled activities were allowed to continue for so many years clearly demonstrates that this did not happen.

Margaret, Albert, Mark and Doris

Returning to the other scenarios presented in Chapter 1, Doris (p. 21) was the young mother who killed her son and paternal grandfather, Albert. Doris was the granddaughter who had been sexually abused by Albert (p. 25). Mark (p. 35) was Doris's husband, who had been violent towards her and who had abandoned her for another woman almost as soon as she became pregnant with their son. Margaret (p. 28) was Doris's maternal grandmother; that is, Doris's mother was the child whom Margaret had physically and emotionally abused.

Left on her own to look after her son and with increasing health problems herself, Doris reluctantly turned to her family for help. Her mother helped her with her son at first, but made it clear that she had never liked or approved of her husband Mark and that she had known that Doris's leaving home to live with him was a mistake. She had never shown Doris much affection, and while she had never been quite as brutal to Doris as her own mother Margaret had been to her, she was a very strict and unforgiving woman. As Doris's health deteriorated, so they turned to other family members to share in the care of her son. Not surprisingly, given that he had already abused several other children, Albert was only too keen to offer his help with his great-grandchild, an offer that was warmly received by all concerned, except Doris. Doris had never mentioned the fact that her grandfather had sexually abused her ever since she had tried to tell her mother and was then punished for it. Albert's increasing involvement with her own son was a source of terrible distress for Doris, and this is when her 'schizophrenia' began. She began to be very emotionally detached and her appearance deteriorated, as did the cleanliness and tidiness of her home. The family were concerned about her so she went to her doctor, who referred her back to the local psychiatric services. She was already on medication following the period of distress after her son was born and had been hospitalized for a few weeks at that time. Concerned about the deterioration in her health, her lack of emotion and her telegraphic speech, the diagnosis was changed to that of schizophrenia and she was admitted to hospital once more. Since she had a young child, social services became involved and the child was considered for a short-term fostering placement. To avoid this happening, Doris's family offered to look after the boy and, once again, some of this support was to involve Albert.

On the weekend of Doris's release from the psychiatric hospital, Albert was staying in her council house, looking after the property for her while she was away. When Doris returned home her son was brought to her by her mother and Albert was left with them in the house to keep an eye on Doris and see that she was managing all right. Doris was told that the boy had been poorly and that he had had an upset stomach. She began to become more confused and distressed. Doris had never felt comfortable being left with Albert, and even all these years after the abuse had stopped he still had a hold over her. She never felt in control around him and just became very passive and compliant. She felt like a little girl when he was around. She had never let herself believe that Albert would ever abuse her son as well, convincing herself that she was his only victim; that there were no others before or after he had abused her so terribly. But her son's upset stomach was disturbing her, even though she had not consciously made any connection to Albert or possible abuse.

Over the course of her first night home, Doris was unable to sleep and had a restless night. Perhaps she was unconsciously keeping a watchful eye on her son. She listened to the radio that night and heard an account from staff at a children's hospice about working with terminally ill children. They sometimes told the children that they would be with Jesus, and that Jesus loved children and would not let them suffer any more once they were with him. Doris took this to be a sign from God. She became convinced that her son was suffering from a terminally ill condition and that the symptoms he was displaying were those of meningitis. The next day, Doris awoke from a nightmare to find her son's health had deteriorated. He was still complaining of an upset stomach and had a slight temperature. The doctors who had seen him while she had been in hospital were sure it was nothing serious, just a bout of gastric flu. Relatives came and went and found that Doris was becoming withdrawn again and that she seemed concerned about her son being ill. They were not unduly worried about her as they knew that after the weekend she would be back in hospital – besides, they were used to her being a bit strange and not always making sense. That night saw Doris becoming more and more disturbed. Albert's public appearance of gentleness and kindness was a lie and she knew it. At the same time it was very confusing for her because no one could see through it and no one ever suspected anything. It all made her doubt herself, doubt that this was the man who had abused her, just as she had been confused as a little girl.

In the morning Doris woke early to find her son in considerable pain with his stomach. Whether Albert had abused him that night or not was never confirmed, but the fact that he had stomach pains reminded her of her own childhood. In a state of complete confusion between her past and her present she could not bear to see her tiny son suffer any longer. She loved him too much and she literally loved him to death. Crying and telling him she loved him, she put a pillow over his head until he was still. Now he could be with Jesus and now he would never have to suffer in this way again. In a heightened state of emotion and in a further expression of her newly found ability to prevent children from suffering, she went into her grandfather's bedroom in the dark, just as he had done to her all those years ago. She straddled his weak body just as he had straddled hers, and she smothered him with a pillow and stopped him from breathing just as he had done to her. Now she was in control, now she could put a stop to him hurting her or any other children. She left the room, closed the door, and swallowed a bottle of tablets so as to finish what she had started. She was intoxicated when the police found her. All she could tell them was that now they were with Jesus, about meningitis, and about how she had wanted to help.

Peter

Peter grew up with uncertainty and instability as the only constant feature of his childhood. His father had been a Forces man and, as such, was a very strict disciplinarian and very unforgiving of his children's behaviour. He expected even the youngest of his three children to behave like mature adults and any sign of vulnerability had to be dealt with severely; to do anything else would be to bring them up to be soft and weak. For their own good they had to be tough and disciplined and he ran his household like a military barracks. Apart from his father's strict regime, there were other consequences of being a Forces child. One of the most damaging was that about every eighteen months or two years the family were relocated to a different part of the country – on one occasion to Cyprus and on another to Germany. Every move meant a different school, always having to be the new member of an established class, and having to make new friends. There seemed no point in making new friends because they were, like everything else, inevitably impermanent. In total, by the time he was sixteen, Peter had been to twelve different schools. Three days after his sixteenth birthday his father died suddenly of a heart attack. He was just forty-one. Peter's mother died of cancer three years later, and so at nineteen he was effectively orphaned and had to look after himself.

Peter had struggled financially in those first few years after his parents died and had worked incredibly hard wherever he was employed so as to reach a level of financial security. No matter how much money he earned or how comfortable he was financially, he was always certain that it would all be taken away from him. His experiences of instability and loss had left him with a deep and unshakeable conviction that nothing in life was permanent and that just around the corner something would happen to take it all away. So it was at the age of forty-one, with little or no conscious awareness of the fact that this was the age at which his father had suddenly died, Peter found himself overwhelmed by feelings of insecurity and impending doom. Deep down he was convinced that he too would never make it past forty-one. Once again, the past and the present were resonating together so as to lead to strong feelings that Peter was unable to make sense of and that he experienced as distress.

There were other aspects of his present life that were exposing Peter to yet more uncertainty. The company that he worked so hard for was rumoured to be about to be taken over by a large American firm. If the takeover took place there would inevitably be job losses, and Peter's sense of life as impermanent meant that he was convinced that he would be a definite redundancy candidate – more uncertainty and further potential threat. His early experiences meant that he did not cope well with any further uncertainty and his 'symptoms' were the expression of his growing sense of powerlessness and lack of control. He became more irritable, less tolerant of those around him, and because he did not feel in control of his life or his emotions, he attempted to regain his equilibrium by being in control of others. As well as various inanimate objects, those in the immediate firing line included his family and the unfortunate man who had forced him to momentarily lose control of his car.

Derek

Derek was also a child of chaos. He was born into a house of poverty and into an area of deprivation. With a black mother and a white father, his life was never going to be easy in a predominantly white country. His drunken and violent father left his mother when he was only two, so he never knew him.

His mother suffered from a number of illnesses and was unable to work because of this. She had various lovers who came and stayed with her for a while and then they would be gone again. The only men Derek knew as he grew up were transient, and each time that another one appeared on the scene his mother would be distracted and show less interest in him. He grew to associate his mother's boyfriends with periods of loneliness and isolation. His mother was very young when she had him and was not really able to cope with the demands of a young son. She also kept getting involved with violent men who treated her badly and took advantage of her. As a consequence of her ill health and her relative immaturity, she found his behaviour difficult to control and did what she knew best, which was to smack him or grab him by the wrist. The more tired and irritable she became, the less tolerant she was of his behaviour and the more he demanded of her. At times he would bang his head against the floor to gain her attention, and he was always frightened to sleep on his own. When she was without a man in her life, his mother let him sleep in bed with her, but as soon as she had lovers to stay, he would be evicted and the trouble over his sleeping would flare up again.

Derek's behaviour became increasingly unmanageable and he was unable to show any form of concentration at nursery school. He was easily distracted and constantly in need of attention from adults. Due to his poor subsequent performance at infant school and his very obvious emotional and behavioural problems, he was assessed to see if he was in need of specialized help. He performed so poorly in this unfamiliar man's tests that he was assessed as being intellectually well below average. This was the early 1970s, and children who were severely distressed were seen in the same way as children who were handicapped. In either case they were educationally subnormal. On the advice of the school and the local authority, Derek's mother was offered the possibility of sending her son to a boarding school for children with special educational needs. Unable to cope with her son at the best of times, she readily accepted the offer of special help for her son that took him away from her most of the time. So it was at the age of seven that Derek found himself taken

away from his south London home and dumped in a huge build-
ing with 130 children with mild to severe learning difficulties
(in the 1970s they were still called the 'mentally handicapped').

Not only did Derek feel totally confused and abandoned, but
he was surrounded by other boys who could barely speak to
him, many of whom were considerably bigger and older than
he was. He was terrified. This was just the beginning of nine
years of Derek's life that he was later to describe as 'like being
in hell'. There was no formal education whatsoever. In fact,
Derek did not see a book until four years after he arrived. Most
of the classes were unstructured and chaotic. The headteacher
was involved in systematically beating the boys with a cane for
whatever they did; he was in total control of them and they all
feared him. If any child in a dormitory made a noise after lights
out, then all the boys had to line up with their hands held out.
If they moved their hands they were beaten about the body. If
they made a sound they were similarly beaten. At other times
the headteacher and various members of staff would slap the
children about the face without warning, usually for trivial matters such as laughing or speaking too loud. The violence did not
end there.

The headteacher was also involved in systematically sexually
abusing many of the boys. Soon after they arrived they would
be called into his office and be forced to remove their trousers
and pants. He gained their total compliance by first beating their
bare backsides with his cane. After that he would fondle their
buttocks and their penises and get them to perform oral sex on
him. At other times he would gather two or three of the boys
and get them to abuse each other. Since Derek was a mixed-race
child, he seemed to be singled out for especially brutal treatment
from this man. Not only was he beaten more regularly, but he
was also anally abused in the headteacher's office from the age
of eight until he was about twelve. The sexual abuse of the boys
seemed to stop once they reached puberty. Some of the many
boys who had been sexually abused carried out the same violence on the younger boys as they arrived new to the school.
Derek was at times anally abused by the older boys in his dormitory soon after arriving there. He never told anyone at home

what was happening; he was simply too terrified to do so. The best he could do was to cry and sob every time he had to return there from home at the end of the holidays, but his mother ignored this and sent him on his way.

Even when he had left the school his mother made it quite clear that she had her own life and he was not really wanted at her home. In any case, she could barely afford to pay for him as well and she resented the fact that he was not working. Derek spent the next few years leaving home for a few months and then returning again for brief spells. Each time he returned home he hoped his mother would be pleased to see him, but she was not for very long. Most of the time they did not get on particularly well. He was unable to maintain any form of work because as soon as he spent any time in a job he began to become frightened of his workmates' friendliness towards him. He found it too difficult to trust anyone, so he would leave. Much of the time he spent homeless on the streets or in hostels. It was at this time that he discovered that drink made him feel more confident and he very quickly developed a dependency on alcohol.

On the evening of the stabbing there had been a terrible and almost fatal misunderstanding. Derek and his new friend had each misinterpreted the other's friendliness and interest. The older man was gay and he did not think he was being invited back to Derek's house just to drink whisky. For his part, Derek was completely unable to understand the signals that this man was giving him. He had no concept of sexuality and no idea about the differences between friendliness and sexual advances. More than this, without any awareness on his part, there was something about his manner that was inappropriate and sexual, especially when he had been drinking. All the same, he had no idea of the other man's intentions and was just quietly pleased to have someone he could take home and thereby show his mother that he did have friends.

After they had drunk the whisky the older man began to touch Derek and to try and kiss him. Derek froze; he was petrified. Once again he found himself in a situation that for so many years as a child he had been powerless to do anything about.

The older man did not understand Derek's passivity and took it to mean that he was shy. Derek's head began to spin and his heart began to pound faster and faster. He felt young and helpless and very scared. The past and the present merged together. All he could do was recall the pain and the suffering that he feared was about to happen to him again, and that he felt he could do nothing whatsoever to stop. The older man tried to encourage him by speaking to him and reassuring him, still having no idea how Derek was feeling. Suddenly Derek panicked completely. He ran into the kitchen and picked up a kitchen knife. All he wanted to do was to scare the man, to regain some control over the situation, and to make him stop. When he entered the room the other man was completely surprised that he was wielding a knife and started to shout at him, telling him he was crazy and what the hell was he up to. Derek was barely listening to him by this stage. All he could see was an older man shouting at him angrily and coming towards him. He lunged out and stabbed him. The fact that he attacked the man with a knife was not a random or senseless act. Derek could have hit out or threatened the man with any form of blunt or heavy object. Instead, without any conscious awareness on his part, he chose a method of defence that involved bodily penetration. He could not explain to anyone why he had acted the way he had done because he himself had no idea why. In any case, he had never told anyone what had happened to him. All he could do was hint to the world through his actions.

·5·

Troubled Children, Troubled Adults

Closely allied to the myth that violent or distressed people are born and not made is the commonly held belief that troubled, difficult or distressed children emerge from the womb already predisposed to such characteristics. The notion that children are born wild or savage, or in some way inherently bad or evil, has in many ways softened over the course of the twentieth century. Yet this belief still implicitly pervades many contemporary beliefs about children and childhood, and it resurfaces whenever there is a high-profile case in the media involving child per-petrators. This ideology has come in various guises and has had profound implications for how childhood has been viewed this century, and for the ways in which we make sense of children as they develop. One of the implications of this basic assumption was the view that children should be treated strictly with at times harsh discipline, so as to avoid them developing into adults who have no self-control or who are at the mercy of their basic animal instincts. These beliefs were for a long time embedded within an essentially religious framework, and driven by the imperative to 'tame' children, so much cruelty and suffering has been handed out to so many children. The consequences of this have been quite literally to brutalize children through fear and often violent punishment, rather than offering love, guidance and encouragement; it has created generations of adults who have not only been 'God fearing', but frightened of themselves as well as of other people.

Talking to many parents in the course of my work, I often get the impression that they genuinely believe that nurturing children with love, sympathy and kindness is something that should be avoided at all costs since this will lead to them being spoilt, clingy and weak-willed, and therefore poorly equipped as adults to cope with the harsh realities of life. In truth, it is those fortunate children who are genuinely wanted, loved, nurtured and encouraged, and who develop in conditions of relative stability, who will have at least some chance of coping with the inherent uncertainties that they will face in the modern world.

For decades, the popular belief about children who were put 'in care' was that were removed from home because these particular children were in some way or another bad. Thus these children used to be referred to as 'juvenile delinquents', and in many ways they are still viewed simplistically as out-of-control trouble-makers. The reality, however, is that in most cases these children have been removed from home through circumstances and experiences that were not their fault, and over which they had little or no control. Many children have been taken into care (or children's homes) because one or other of their parents has died or because their parents themselves did not want to, or were unable to, cope with looking after them. Some children will be removed from their homes because their behaviour poses a threat or has become unmanageable in other ways, but often the mistake is made of failing to see this as a response and adaptation to their experiences and to their environment: these are in many cases the children of chaos.

Children who are profoundly distressed and disturbed by abuse, instability and neglect are in most cases taken away from 'home' for their own protection: because their home environment has been deemed by the local authorities to be unsafe or unsustainable in the interest of the child's (or other people's) welfare. However, the situation at home has to have become unsustainable, or else the children have to have been abused or neglected for social services and the legal system to decide that the state is in a better position to look after them than their parents or relatives. Social services departments are over-stretched and, like many other public bodies, under-resourced, particularly in the area of child protection; at the same time, however, there are ever-increasing numbers of disturbed, distressed and violent children. Therefore, the threshold for what constitutes a child 'at risk' is constantly shifting and having to be redefined to encompass those children who are considered to be most vulnerable to harm. There are thus many children who will, like Robert Thompson and Jon Venables, inevitably 'slip through the net' without receiving the help or protection they so desperately need.

Despite the inconsistent collection of data (and at times lack of it) by local education authorities, it has also been estimated that young people 'in care' make up 33 percent of all exclusions in secondary school and 66 percent of primary school exclusions.[1] Some of these children who are put into care do indeed behave in ways that are impulsive, aggressive and out of control and they are unable to accept much, if any, responsibility for their actions. A number of them will be violent and some will add significantly to the general crime statistics as well. Among their number are the 'juvenile delinquents' so beloved of successive Home Secretaries, who find them useful targets for flexing their moral and political muscles. The reality of these children's and adolescents' lives is all too often a picture of abuse, neglect and chaos. It is hard to see how a child can develop a sense of morality or a sense of personal responsibility, or to co-operate with and respect others, when they have grown up in a totally immoral adult world, one where no one has taken any responsibility for them and where they have been shown little or no respect or care. It is just as hard to understand how they are to develop a sense of control over their own actions when their lives have been characterized by an almost total lack of control over what happens to them, over their relationships, over where they reside or for how long. Equally, it is hard to see how they are supposed to develop a sense of empathy with others and to take into account other people's feelings when no one has afforded them the same respect. To expect these human values (or the absence of them) to be innate is like expecting a child in an English-speaking country to grow up fluent in Chinese.

The very systems that have for decades been given the responsibility of looking after children who have been removed from home have systematically failed many of the youngsters in their care. If the children were not already damaged by the experiences that led them into the care system, then many have been harmed or even brutalized by the very people and places that were supposed to be protecting them from further harm. For one thing, these children will in many cases grow up and spend most of their time with other very distressed and disturbed children. As childhood and particularly adolescence is a crucial period for the development of a person's identity, the impact of the absence of a consistent relative or family unit is beyond measure. Relationships with substitute carers, such as staff in residential units, and with the peer group are therefore critical because they form the replacement for a family. Obviously in care settings, especially residential units, the peer group will inevitably consist of other children who have been abused and excluded from mainstream society. Therefore relationships with other children as well as care staff are beset with problems from the outset.

Most residential care units are unfortunately all too often cauldrons of mistrust, confusion and instability. Relationships are all too often characterized by violence and hatred, bullying and intimidation, intolerance, impulsiveness and confusion, involving many young people who feel bad about themselves, who feel abandoned, and who have little or no experience of being cared for. Children in such units will quickly learn to size each other up and a dominance hierarchy will develop. There will always be those who remain relatively passive and easily led, often as an attempt to impress or to please their peers or to avoid being bullied, while others will – through intimidation and aggression – control and abuse the other children in the unit. Also, relationships with other children who also are moving in and out of the care system or to other units will, as with all previous relationships, be characterized by impermanence and instability.

If children look to the staff who look after them for models of relationships, they will all too often be disappointed. Most care workers are poorly trained or have no training at all, and the staff turnover in such units is typically very high, so that once again the relationship with many of these adults is also transient. On top of this, such units are routinely understaffed, poorly managed, and the staff badly paid. Reflecting the wider cultural attitudes towards these children, care staff themselves will generally be split into those who are essentially punitive in outlook and those who see their role as one of possible rehabilitation. Many staff see care work as simply a job like any other and are frequently and steadfastly punitive in their outlook; ignorant of the special needs of the children with whom they have been entrusted, they see their task as basically controlling the 'bad' children in their care. Others who work in the same homes are much kinder in outlook and see their role in terms of genuinely trying to care for and to help the children in their overall development. In this way, almost all the care and residential units I have come across that deal with troubled children are characterized by a tension between control on the one hand and rehabilitation on the other. More often than not, they simply contain the children until it is time for them to leave when they reach eighteen or when they can be housed elsewhere. The staff, as well as the children themselves, may frequently be at risk of aggression or assault by other children, partly because the regimes are often based on punishment and control (therefore confrontations are routine), and partly because the children's behaviour is, in the majority of instances, very demanding. In any case, children in care stand a far greater risk of being harmed by those unscrupulous members of staff who have gravitated towards working with vulnerable children as an excuse to abuse them.

Children living away from home: the failure of care

We are only slowly beginning to realize the extent to which we have failed generations of vulnerable children through a system of state 'care' that has not only failed to protect them, but that has inflicted further harm upon them. Britain has as a society systematically betrayed its most vulnerable children for over forty years. Since the Second World War, hundreds and thousands of distressed and troubled children have been put into various forms of residential care. Up and down the country the casualties of various residential settings where children were living 'away from home' are at last coming forward and are able to have their experiences of abuse and betrayal finally believed. For decades, children who had been removed from their original homes have been placed in circumstances where they were further abused by those whose responsibility it was to look after them, and where over the same period of time their complaints were systematically ignored.

Since the 1950s, more children than ever before in British history have been removed from their familial homes and placed under the care of the state. Having been removed from their homes for various reasons, whether they were considered unmanageable or out of control, or whether they were simply unwanted, orphaned and with nowhere else to go, they were placed in institutions that were not only experimental and untested, but wholly based on the particular notions of childhood and society that were in force at the time. The 'approved schools' of the 1950s – which at their peak housed some 8,000 children, some as young as eight years old – were boarding schools for so called 'delinquents' that pathetically mimicked the fee-paying public school system. Almost all the children in them came from deprived backgrounds or broken homes characterized by familial discord instability and violence. Many of these institutions became harsh, brutal places in which the children were treated to constant physical punishment and bullying either from staff or from older boys. Greystone Heath was an approved school for boys in Warrington, and for years was seen as a model institution. From 1965 onwards dozens of boys were subjected to rape and physical assault by a group of men whose countless crimes would not be dealt with until decades later. Following a scandal at Court Leas approved school in Surrey, which in 1968 revealed horrific levels of violence and physical punishment, the approved schools began to be closed down.

Then came the Youth Treatment centres of the 1970s, based upon naïve medical and psychological models about the nature of difficult children. These young people were seen as requiring 'treatment'; as a result, they were not only medicated, but also subjected to simplistic behaviourist programmes or attempts at group therapy. All too often these systems degenerated into the regular use of violence and systems of restraint by naïve and poorly trained staff who, though well intentioned, had little or no experience in dealing with severely distressed children. Then came the brutal Borstal systems of the 1970s and the early 1980s, based upon harsh notions of military discipline. At the same time the number of children being looked after by the state increased dramatically, and social services and local authority residential units were set up throughout the 1980s to cope with the burgeoning demand for placements for troubled children.

It is only since the beginning of the 1990s that there has been a widespread emergence of allegations of physical, emotional and sexual abuse in children's homes throughout the 1950s to 1980s throughout Wales, Scotland and England. As I write, there are currently eighteen police investigations taking place following a number of high-profile cases in Staffordshire (over 140 children were abused over a six-year period leading to £2 million compensation in 1991), Leicestershire, North and South Wales (at least thirty-three homes are still under investigation), Sunderland, Cheshire, Manchester, Merseyside, Edinburgh, Northumbria and London. The terrible failures of a national system of 'care' are at last emerging, a system that was set up to protect our most vulnerable children and that is now being exposed as having been riddled with abuse and abusers, or as having had regimes that were in many cases consistently cruel. Hundreds of detailed and substantive complaints and allegations were made for decades and yet, as has so often been the case, these complaints were met by a culture of disbelief: doctors, health visitors, the police, social workers and the social services inspectorate all failed to take seriously what they were being told. Sir William Utting, a former Chief Inspector of Social Services, was asked by the then Conservative government to lead an inquiry into the safeguards against abuses faced by children living away from home, either in local authority care, at boarding school or in other institutions.[2] The report that was made public in November 1997 prompted the Health Secretary to comment that it was 'a woeful tale of failure at all levels to provide a secure and decent childhood for some of the most vulnerable children'.[3] The report highlights how young children who for decades had been complaining of abuse were not believed, and in many cases sent back to the homes. When they ran away this was seen as further evidence of their deviance and they were then returned to their abusers.

Even though the overwhelming majority of child sex offenders operate in secrecy and isolation, the scandal of children's homes in North Wales provides a disturbing insight into the potential size of the problem, as well as the difficulty in uncovering sexual abuse and prosecuting the abusers. After twenty-seven police inquiries failed to uncover the extent of the problem, thirteen unpublished social services reports, a major police inquiry in 1991, and another unpublished report by Clwyd County Council, allegations about seven residential homes in Clwyd, North Wales, where some 300 children were physically and sexually abused over a twenty-year period, are now the focus of a public inquiry. Police have interviewed 2,500 people and received over 500 complaints of abuse from hundreds of men and women who were in care and have come forward. Accusations have been levelled at as many as 148 men, but so far only eight have been prosecuted with six of them actually being convicted. The elaborate systems of deceit and the extent to which the sexual abuse and rape of children has taken place rivals any major international drug smuggling cartel and would leave even the most hardened conspiracy theorists shocked. Policemen, social workers, probation officers, local authority executives and at least a dozen prominent public figures and businessmen have all been accused and implicated in the systematic and widespread sexual abuse of children and the infiltration of children's homes that has taken place over many decades in North Wales. Several of those adults who have given evidence have died under suspicious circumstances.

The initial findings of the tribunal demonstrate the level at which such operations can take place: many of those involved had previously been accused but exonerated, some on as many as four previous occasions. Some of those who had been exonerated went on to be convicted of sexual offences against children, but only once they had moved to another part of the country where they were no longer shielded by a network of powerful associates. Disturbingly for those who would insist that the evidence is too disturbing or too far-fetched to be real, or indeed that accusations have been made for reasons of vendetta or revenge, is that a picture of corroborated evidence has begun to emerge: several of those who have been named have been named independently by different witnesses, and several of those prominent figures who were named had indeed been subsequently convicted of sexual offences against children after the original abuses had taken place.

The Utting report reviewed fifty previously unpublished Department of Health studies into the abuse of children in residential homes and schools. Two-thirds of the abused children were boys and two-thirds of the abuse was sexual. Of the forty-eight abusers, fifteen had come under suspicion on previous occasions and, astonishingly, three of them had previous convictions. Some sex offenders had amassed literally hundreds of victims over a lifetime 'career' of abuse. The report also found that the perpetrators of abuse were frequently in positions of power, responsibility, authority and trust, and were also likely to have been in their jobs for at least five years. Peter Righton was a highly influential consultant in child care who lectured in many colleges across Britain. By the time he was finally convicted for abusing boys, he had become the Director of Education at the Institute of Social Work in London, a position that enabled him to have some influence on government policy. Keith

Laverack, one of the original members of the paedophile ring at Greystone Heath approved school in the 1960s, was in charge of the Guardian ad Litem panel for Cambridgeshire County Council. This meant that he was responsible for representing the interests of children in court cases, a position that gave him access to countless vulnerable children in the area and information on abused children throughout the country. Roger Saint assaulted countless children in his foster care over many years in North Wales. By the time he was caught and convicted he was a member of the local adoption panel, which was responsible for dealing with complaints about child abuse.

After her conviction for manslaughter in 1968, Mary Bell was sent to Red Bank Special Unit in Merseyside for five years before being transferred to a maximum security women's prison at the age of sixteen. For almost the whole duration of that five years at Red Bank, Mary was the only girl among twenty boys. Not only did she receive no therapeutic care during that time, but she was also systematically abused. According to other inmates who were resident with Mary at that time, one member of staff subjected her to repeated attacks and she was also abused by fellow residents. Certain members of staff actively encouraged the abuse through their obvious disapproval of her – they even instructed the male residents not to call her Mary. When she arrived she was not segregated in any way despite being the only girl, and the male residents routinely abused her sexually.

In 1970, at the age of thirteen, Mary complained that she had been sexually abused by a housemaster at Red Bank, but a judge refused to believe her story. Yet again, as had happened so many times throughout her life, her attempts to draw attention to and to stop what was happening to her went dismissed and unheard. Only thirty years later is there an investigation taking place after the police have admitted that they are looking into the abuse of residents at Red Bank over several decades and that further arrests are still possible. The teacher who is alleged to have abused Mary has not been traced and is said to be dead. After four years of the investigation and hundreds of statements from former residents at Red Bank, Mary herself has not yet been interviewed. She was finally released into the community at the age of twenty-three, 'under licence' as a Schedule One offender. As it had done for so many others, the system of state care had completely failed Mary, leaving her poorly equipped to cope with life, emotionally confused, and with virtually no experiences of benign relationships. Having been maltreated virtually throughout her period of detainment, the state-run institutions that were responsible for her thus continued to systematically subject her to many of the conditions that led to her crime and detainment in the first place. It is interesting to note that Mary's recent disclosures of her experience of abuse have been met with the predictable response of suspicion and disbelief. Comments have been repeatedly made in the media casting doubt on Mary's disclosures about her pre-1968 experiences of abuse (at the hands of her mother and her mother's 'customers'). Similar dismissive remarks have been made about the abuse she was subjected to while in care – despite the corroboration from other residents who were also in care with her verifying what happened, and despite the police's disclosure that they were indeed investigating substantial allegations of institutional abuse at Red Bank at the time that she was resident there.

It is not only in the statutory or 'official' institutions for dealing with distressed and vulnerable children that society has systematically failed to look after those youngsters who are living 'away from home'. The Christian Brothers, one of the largest orders of Roman Catholic society which once ran 100 schools and orphanages in Ireland, took the unprecedented step of publishing an apology in Irish newspapers on 28 March 1998. The adverts apologize for the physical and sexual abuse inflicted on Irish pupils and orphans following a series of substantiated abuse cases, many of which went back several decades. The adverts admit the almost systematic use of harsh punishments. At almost the same time as these apologies appeared in Irish newspapers, suspended priest Rudolph Kos was convicted of systematically sexually abusing altar boys in Dallas in the United States, in a case in 1997 that led to a record £71 million damages against the Roman Catholic Church.

In 1998 National Children's Homes Action for Children, a charity that once ran some fifty children's homes and schools in the 1960s–1980s, came under the ever-widening spotlight when some of its former employees were convicted of abusing children in their homes. Following a prior conviction of four employees in one of its Cheshire homes, Robert Starr was sentenced to fifteen years in prison for offences against boys under his 'care' in South Wales. Further allegations are still under investigation. When the scandals about abuse in children's homes began to emerge, several insurance companies realized the potential extent of the compensation claims that they might face and threatened to withdraw their cover if the succession of inquiry findings continued to be made public. It is indeed a sign of the times if the duty to adequately protect vulnerable children in care is only taken seriously because local authorities fear the economic repercussions of not doing so.

The systematic sexual exploitation of children is not restricted to those who are especially vulnerable because they are effectively parentless and living away from home. Following the conviction in 1998 of four men who admitted abusing young boys, the police investigation into the breakaway Scout Group, the Baden-Powell Scouts Association, found that as many as 300 boys have been abused over the last few decades. Some 4,000 photos and videos in one of the men's houses were found with at least fifty unidentified boys having been filmed or photographed. The organization was found to be at the centre of a huge paedophile network with nationwide connections to several major British cities and also to Europe.

In 1997 it was announced that a national network of up to eight separate jails to hold offenders under the age of eighteen was to be set up by the Home Office after the Chief Inspector of Prisons produced a report condemning the treatment of the 2,600 teenagers in Britain's young offender institutes and adult prisons.[4] Sir David Ramsbotham, the author of the report, was so disturbed by the conditions that he discovered that he made it clear that the prison service was a totally inappropriate place to detain children, and that such treatment would serve to damage them further and increase the likelihood of them reoffending. Commenting on these conditions he wrote: 'They [the conditions] are, in many cases, far below the minimum conditions

---

in Social Services Department secure units required by the Children Act (1989) and the UN Convention on the Rights of the Child.'[5] The report comments on the 'chasm of low self-esteem' held by these teenagers and the fact that the vast majority of them needed individual attention for the underlying problems that produced their criminal behaviour in the first place, rather than 'being stored in a warehouse' (the report highlights the fact that behind the 'masculine bravado', many of the young prisoners had been the victims of sexual and physical abuse). Another report, *Violent Victims*, surveyed Section 53 offenders, a group of ten- to seventeen-year-olds who are detained under the Children and Young Persons Act 1933.[6] The report found that almost three-quarters of these young offenders had experienced some form of childhood abuse, and frequently it was many or even all forms of abuse. The majority of these young offenders were male, and a small proportion of them had attacked or killed their abusers.

In 1998 it is estimated that there are some 200,000 children in Britain who live away from home in some form of residential unit, institution or, increasingly, foster care. The number of residential placements or children's homes has fallen dramatically over recent years as there has been a massive ideological shift in favour of fostering. The Utting report recommended that the widespread increase in private foster agencies should be the subject of greater protection. The report suggests, however, that the abuse of foster children is on the increase and that determined sex offenders are now targeting other areas – in particular, foster care and boarding schools. Inevitably, with large numbers of children being switched to foster care from residential units there will be, as there already have been, foster family scandals and systematic abuse of children by certain foster parents; the case of Roger Saint is evidence enough of this. I myself have worked with many adults who were abused when they were in either temporary or permanent foster care.

According to the Utting report, we are supposed to be reassured that because there are now much more thorough safeguards in place, such systematic and widespread abuse is unlikely to occur again. However, the fact that Utting echoes the reassurances of previous reports may indicate that such assurances in the past have been false. Despite the assurances, inquiries, scandals, reports, investigations and the compensation claims, Sir Herbert Lamming, Chief Inspector of Social Services, said in April 1998 that safeguards against abuse of young people in care remains 'at best patchy and in some places wholly unacceptable'.[7] In other words, there will be many more children abused while 'in care', and so yet more children for whom the system fails to offer protection. It is not a question of whether more children who live 'away from home' will be abused or not, but whether they will speak of their experiences and whether they will be believed when they do.

Sir William Utting, commenting on his report, said that, '[These children] must take their place among other priorities for increased public expenditure . . . The ultimate cost to society of not doing these things will be many times greater through the burden of ruined adult lives.'[8] The report presents evidence of high levels of ill health among children in care, estimating that 75 percent of them had mental health problems. One professor of medicine who gave evidence commented that they were the most deprived children he had ever met, and that the majority had serious physical or mental health problems.

The cost to society is indeed a high one. The figure, for example, of educating an excluded child is twice that of keeping them in mainstream education (and, as we have seen, children in care make up a significant proportion of those who are excluded from school). If such youngsters drift into a pattern of crime and offending (as many of them do), a place in a young offenders' unit costs about £500 per week per child; and if they offend in a manner that leads to their detention in a secure unit, this can cost as much as £3,000 per week per child.

Yet despite the inadequacies and the failures over many decades of countless residential units, young offenders' units and detention centres to rehabilitate children, or even protect them, the political response to the growing tide of distressed children has been unimaginative and predictable. The latest version of units for young offenders, known as Youth Training Centres, will be used to detain up to forty twelve- to fourteen-year-old persistent offenders for anywhere between three months and a maximum of a year. The first of these was opened in Medway in Kent in 1998. The cost of these units will be a staggering £260,000 a year per child; that is, £5,000 per week per child.

The overall cost to society once these distressed children leave statutory care is impossible to quantify and would be meaningless if just seen in economic terms. Poorly equipped to cope with life in mainstream society, many with severe social and health problems, those leaving care have for years received little or no after-care support. Many of them will leave poorly socialized and, because they have frequently been treated so badly, they will be mistrustful of statutory agencies to the extent that they will find it hard to accept any support even were it to be offered. Even today there is still little after-care follow-up and virtually no support in the community for care leavers. The Utting report also highlighted the fact that for many years basic records have not been kept, so many children could (and have) literally disappeared from official society and 'gone missing'. The fate of so many of Fred West's victims, many of whom (including Rose West herself) were care leavers, went undetected for years precisely because once they left the system they ceased to receive any statutory support or monitoring. Seven of the ten of Fred's victims were care leavers, as had been two of the main three survivors. Social services had no records of where they went after they left care and no record of Cromwell Street.

The long-term outcome for children once they have left care makes for depressing reading: three out of four care leavers have no academic qualifications; over half become unemployed immediately; one in six female care leavers is pregnant by age sixteen or seventeen; a third of young, single homeless people have been in care; 40 per cent of young people in prison have been in care; and a quarter of the adult prison population has been in care.[9] Given the links between distress, violence and childhood abuse, which is one of the principal focuses of this book, it should come as no surprise to learn that many care leavers will end up in the strange and brutal world of the maximum security 'special' hospitals.

The 'special' hospitals

In 1992 I began working as a clinical psychologist in Rampton Hospital. Rampton is one of three maximum security 'special' hospitals found in England, the other two being Ashworth and Broadmoor, with Carstairs being the one Scottish equivalent. Patients at the special hospitals are detained under the Mental Health Act (1983) on account of their having been diagnosed as having a mental disorder, as defined by the Act, and also because of the level of danger they are assessed as posing. Since these large institutions are associated with the detention of several very high-profile killers such as Ian Brady, Peter Sutcliffe and Beverley Allitt, the public perception of these places is that all of the people who are detained there are dangerous killers. In fact, though it may seem strange, many of the patients have not actually committed an offence at all. While a proportion have been convicted of violent crimes, including manslaughter, various degrees of physical assault, sexual offences and arson, you need only pose a sufficient threat to yourself or to others to be detained under the Act. This is the only area under British law where *potential* crime can be taken into account: that is, the concept of dangerousness, which is assessed predominantly by psychiatrists and, increasingly, psychologists as well.

Much of the Mental Health Act refers to people with learning disabilities (who used to be referred to as the 'mentally handicapped'), who also make up a significant proportion of patients in these hospitals – again, regardless of whether or not they have actually committed an offence. Until recently, there were many such patients who had been detained for no reason other than their handicap itself. Since they became so institutionalized and there was nowhere else for them to be placed, they have remained in special hospitals for decades, living proof of a society's shifting definitions of dangerous people. But for most people, the special hospitals are perceived as the places where you are sent if you are mad, bad and very dangerous.

According to their objectives under the Mental Health Act, the 'specials' are supposed to *treat* people for their mental disorders as well as to keep them away from the public, but in fact a patient's mental health need only be 'maintained' rather than improved. The fact that some patients who are sent there are harmed and deteriorate while they are there does not seem to trouble anyone unduly. All of the inherent contradictions of psychiatry, a profession largely based upon control yet professing to be one of treatment, are magnified tenfold in these institutions. Although they are defined as hospitals offering psychiatric treatment, their principal function is that of security and detainment, and they are run more along the lines of a prison. They are staffed almost entirely by members of the Prison Officers' Association, and even those who are qualified nurses are predominantly members of this union. While a patient may be detained until they are no longer deemed dangerous, which should theoretically correspond in some way to an improvement in their mental disorder, for the most part the period of detainment is related to the seriousness of the offence. However, since certain sections of the Act require Home Office approval before serious offenders can be moved to less secure units, patients can potentially be detained indefinitely. The most serious offenders will never be released. In this sense, since 'sentences' are of indeterminate length, it is far worse to be convicted of (say) manslaughter and sent to a special hospital, than it is to be convicted of murder and sent to prison; at least in prison you have a fixed sentence and an expectation of when you will be released. The cost of keeping a patient at Ashworth, for example, is close to £100,000 a year compared to £22,000 per year on average for each person in prison.

Despite all the rhetoric of treatment and the title of hospitals, for the most part the tensions between therapy and security are not reconcilable and they are essentially places to keep people away from the public. Since they house some of the most dangerous people, this is the level of security and control that is applied to all patients, regardless of the risk they actually pose. By now, it should come as no surprise to the reader to learn that, for me, one of the most striking features of working within a maximum security hospital was the severity of the life histories that I heard. Almost without exception, the patients who had been detained had experienced traumatic and tragic lives. Experiences of sexual abuse, violence, emotional cruelty, neglect, abandonment and, especially, upbringings of 'chaos' was the norm rather than the exception for these patients. Many were inarticulate, badly educated and poorly skilled, and some had been homeless. The majority were from abusive, deprived and fragmented homes, and many had spent most or all of their earlier years in the 'care' system that has been the focus of much of this chapter.

If these hospitals are supposed to be places of 'evil' where demons are contained, then those seeking such entities there will be disappointed. Those detained were just people, in many ways no different from those outside, and no less human because of some of the horrific acts some of them had committed. Some were unreachable because they were so damaged; others were deeply regressed much of the time and moved in and out of periods of severe distress. Still others were full of hatred, mistrust and fear. As the majority of women there had been sexually abused as children, many of them cut and maimed their own bodies as an expression of this. Many of the patients were themselves deeply shocked at having been sent there (after all, they share the same cultural views of these hospitals as everyone else) and terrified of being there, not least because they were scared of other patients and what they might do. Contrary to their image as remorseless and soulless, some were deeply traumatized by their own acts of violence and, in quieter moments, many not only felt deeply ashamed, but also genuinely remorseful for what they had done. I in no way wish to glorify either them or their actions, nor to show any disrespect to their victims or the victims' relatives. However, the violent offences and the distress of those detained could in many cases be readily understood if looked at in the context of their life experiences. If they were only given back their entire life histories, then their violence and their distress could be seen to be a result of constellations of vulnerable, abused, frightened, confused, hating, insecure, mistrustful and fragmented personalities combined with cruel twists of fate and often desperate and hopeless circumstances. Perhaps more than anything else, seeing them as people and not demons meant respecting them for all that they had been through; in so many unacknowledged and unrecognized ways they were just as much victims as the people they had killed or injured.

While some of the patients would benefit from their detainment, literally held securely until enough time had passed for some of their hatred and rage to subside, a significant proportion would eventually leave the hospital in a worse condition than when they arrived. Some of them were without doubt 'untreatable', reflecting not only the paucity of notions of 'treatment' but also the extent to which they were permanently and irrevocably damaged by their life experiences: as such, some of them should quite rightly never be released back into the community for they will, without doubt, reoffend. The ubiquitous use of psychiatric medication which, since it kept many patients sedated, often seemed more for the benefit of the staff than the patients. In addition, many patients would derive limited benefit from the one-dimensional and essentially rationalistic psychological therapies that were on offer.[10]

As in the media and society in general, what went on within the confines of the hospital was a remarkable process of depersonalization and decontextualization. The majority of staff with the responsibility for the 'care' of these patients made little attempt to link their current functioning, their distress or their index offences with any of their previous life experiences. As in their psychiatric reports, they were often stripped of the context within which they had lived and from whence they came. In professional meetings, in discussions about them, in their assessment reports and in every way, they were depersonalized, dehumanized and denied any meaningful connection to their life histories. There was rarely anything more than token acknowledgement of the horrific realities they had been through. These patients became their index offences or their mental illnesses (i.e. they were defined and viewed largely in terms of the violence they had committed or the illness they were supposed to be suffering from). In other words, they were ill or antisocial (or both) because they were biologically abnormal, and they were often seen as biologically abnormal because they had behaved in antisocial or ill (or both) ways. They were blamed for what they had done and they were also blamed for whatever was believed to have happened to them. Importantly, when the patients tried to speak about their life experiences, they were all too often seen as delusional, making it all up, manipulative or blatant liars. Contrary to the assertions made by staff that I heard on many occasions – that the patients were lying about their backgrounds or their own experiences of victimization to somehow manipulate the legal system or to get sympathy – I could not see how such comments were justified. Having a history of (say) child abuse did not in any case elicit any greater degree of sympathy from staff, whether or not it was validated by the patients' records. Nor are there any legal benefits to be gained by claiming to have been the victim of such experiences.[11] While the experience of victimization and abuse is routinely seen by the public (and, sadly, too many professionals as well) as merely an excuse, such excuses are meaningless unless they offer the person some tangible benefit, which in practice they do not. I often still find that to offer any kind of alternative perspective or a more humane understanding of the violent actions of offenders is often met with disbelief, professional derision and even moral condemnation; such an understanding as I am attempting to offer in this book as an *explanation* is all too readily confused with understanding as *condonement*.

The professional processes of depersonalizing these patients by dismissing their life experiences is important because it leads to a general culture of blame and inhumanity. Just as important, however, is the profound implications these processes have for any debate about nature versus nurture. The extremity of the marginalization of life experiences by the psychiatric profession within the confines of the special hospitals illuminates so clearly the shaky ground upon which psychiatry in general is based. Here are a group of people, many of whom have had the worst life histories imaginable. Given that many have been in 'care', it is not only their word about their experiences of violence and neglect that needs to be believed. As we have seen throughout this chapter, the failure of much of this system is now well enough documented for it to be impossible to deny that at least some of these patients who were in care were routinely abused. If these patients, who have had such profoundly malign experiences of the world, are still treated and viewed as biological aberrations, then we stand no chance whatsoever of differentiating them from those for whom the contribution of their genetic or biological make-up is genuinely more significant. If indeed such people do exist – those who are violent despite genuinely and overwhelmingly benign life experiences and for whom there is no other organic explanation (such as poisoning or head injury) – I have yet to come across them. However, if we invalidate the brutalizing experiences of those who *have* suffered greatly, then we stand no chance of ever finding those individuals (if they do exist at all) who do have chromosomally violent tendencies.

To depersonalize people in this way – to deny them their humanity, regardless of what they themselves have done – is one of the worst forms of violence we are capable of. If those who are doing the depersonalizing also have power over those they have stripped of their humanity, then these are conditions that throughout history have legitimized the worst forms of brutality, violence and genocide. This is the same process that legitimized the 'Final Solution' in Nazi Germany by denying Jews and other groups their status as humans; this same process justified widespread annihilation of indigenous people in Australia and in North and South America; it is the same process that enables those in political conflicts to define their energies as legitimate targets for slaughter; this is the same process that underpins racism and all other forms of discrimination. This process in the special hospitals inevitably found fertile conditions from which to develop into the repeated brutalities that have occurred within their closeted wards. Just as for so many of the institutions that were set up to 'deal' with distressed and difficult children, the specials have suffered from the same forms of violence and malpractice – once again, most of which did not come to light until they were exposed by various public inquiries. Many of the cases of institutional violence have involved the same ingredients: relative powerlessness of the residents who were routinely disbelieved when they complained, the relative isolation of professional practices from the mainstream, their remote location, their relative privacy and their unaccountability.[12]

In 1980 the Boynton report revealed widespread physical brutalities and intimidation by staff on patients at Rampton, which
eventually led to ten nursing staff being convicted of maltreatment.[13] In 1992 a public inquiry was held into patient care at
Ashworth.[14] The report upheld most of the 120 complaints of
serious maltreatment of patients who endured a decade of brutality, abuse and 'a climate of fear' by nursing staff. Prior to the
inquiry, none of these complaints had been upheld by internal
hospital investigations. Sir Louis Blom-Cooper, who chaired the
report, wrote of a culture within the hospital of denigration and
devaluing of patients; that a vivid picture had emerged of life
in a brutalizing, stagnant, closed institution. He commented
that, 'our wider inquiry revealed a hospital environment and
culture which gave rise to numerous incidents arising from an
uncaring and demeaning attitude towards patients',[15] and that
'such has been the low standard of much patient care at Ashworth, the hospital must be a prime candidate to be included
as one of the establishments to be visited in the near future by
the Committee for the Prevention of Torture and Inhuman or
Degrading Treatment or Punishment'.[16] Racism was common
among some staff who singled out blacks and gays for special
brutality. When other staff spoke about the abuses that were
going on, they received offensive material and death threats.
There were several key witnesses, collectively known as the 'Ashworth Five', who submitted crucial evidence to the committee
for inquiry. Dr Gravett commented that, 'we have endured a
repressive, intimidating, anti-therapeutic culture over the
years'.[17] Moira Potier, a clinical psychologist who subsequently
received an MBE for 'services to the NHS', echoed some of
what I had experienced and seen at Rampton during my time
there: '. . . women in Ashworth are controlled, suppressed, . . .
their overwhelming experience is that they are treated like children. They are almost constantly emotionally abused and at
times physically abused. It is my observation that they feel
chronically frightened and overwhelmingly powerless, and that
they are unable to do anything substantial to alter their lot'.[18]
In a separate paper she wrote that, 'a maximally secure environment such as Ashworth Hospital, with its emphasis on authority

and control, the implicit negative theoretical models used by care staff, and its acceptance of conformity as "cure", is a highly ambivalent place in which to nurture real personality development as the outcome of "treatment"'.[19] At the time of writing, Ashworth has come under scrutiny once again as a girl of eight is alleged to have been taken into the hospital by a former patient and left unsupervised with a convicted sex offender. There were alleged brutalities by staff on handicapped patients while I was at Rampton in 1992 and 1993, none of which were upheld by internal investigations. These institutions are beyond reform. Countless people have called for their closure and the need to replace them with much smaller, more progressive and more accountable units. I can only add my voice to theirs and hope that this happens before the next inquiry.

Public myths, private realities

As we have seen, the process of denying all violent offenders their humanity by demonizing them is not of course confined to professionals and ignorant professions. This particular view, allied closely to a general culture of individual blame and culpability, is rapidly reaching frenzied proportions in Britain as we approach the millennium. Various forms of compassion and understanding are being systematically denied the possibility of legitimate expression on a scale that is deeply disturbing. The one group of people who have been singled out for particular depersonalization and who have become our 'contemporary witches' are paedophiles. The climate of simplistic morality about people who sexually offend against children means that little distinction is made between those who download child pornography from the Internet and those who abuse and kill children. It is right that there should be a sense of public outrage and anger about violent crimes, particularly where children are involved, and it is a heartening sign that enough people still care about what happens to those around them.

However, the increasing levels of public condemnation and feverish witch-hunts are both misleading and unhelpful. As well as reflecting the increasingly brutal tide of public morality, they misrepresent and distort the realities of child abuse in particular and of violence in general. More than this, as we have seen throughout history, such views are also dangerous. As an indication of the hardening of public attitudes and the erosion of social cohesion, Gitta Sereny, commenting on her contrasting experiences of the trial, conviction and sentencing of Robert Thompson and Jon Venables with that of Mary Bell which took place in Newcastle some twenty-six years earlier, wrote that: 'It is, I think, of considerable significance in comparison of these two cases, in terms of their nature and the place and time in which they occurred, that while Mary Bell's extended family stood firm in mutual support throughout and after these events, Jon Venables's parents and Robert Thompson's mother were deserted by practically all their relatives and most of their friends.'[20] The relatives of the two boys have also been given new names and, along with their remaining children, rehoused in distant council estates.

Indeed, the recent furore surrounding Mary Bell is further indication of how intolerant and lacking in compassion collective frameworks in Britain have become. The coverage of Mary Bell's original trial in 1968 received little of the sensationalism that we saw over the death of James Bulger, crowds did not gather baying for blood, and the process of mystification was not nearly as intense. There was no outcry following her initial release into the community in 1980 and, albeit with some difficulty, she established a 'normal' life for herself – with a steady long-term relationship and a teenage daughter of her own – demonstrating in her own way that people can triumph over adversity, no matter how terrible that may have been, and that some can indeed by 'rehabilitated'.

Public and media outrage erupted over the publication in May 1998 of Gitta Sereny's latest book about Mary Bell and her life, *Cries Unheard*, and especially that Mary has been paid for her contribution to the book.[21] The media response was to hound her out of her home, and she and her fourteen-year-old daughter had to flee into police protection from the pursuing pack. The media came close to identifying her new identity and location despite still being barred from doing so by a High Court injunction. The hypocrisy of the media reached new heights: the very same newspapers that hounded Mary and her daughter out of their seaside home, and who declared headline outrage at her payment for helping with the book, are the same newspapers that have persistently pursued her for over a decade around the country from one place of hiding to another, offering her large sums of money for her story. Mary was forced by these events to discuss her past with her daughter. Once again, the same all too familiar processes of demonization have taken hold. Instead of public condemnation being tempered by a sense of compassion for Mary's own suffering, the level of debate has been morally one-dimensional. The outrage over her payment for a book that sheds a great deal of understanding about Mary's crimes in 1968 has obscured the importance of the insights that the book has to offer.

Child killers and paedophiles Robert Oliver and Sidney Cooke were part of a ring of sex offenders who abducted, raped and killed fourteen-year-old Jason Swift, as well as Barry Lewis and Mark Tildeseley, during an organized assault at a flat in the East End. They were convicted of manslaughter and not murder due to a lack of evidence, much to the frustration of the police who were also unable to bring charges relating to six other boys whom they believed were also killed by this ring. Following his release after eight years in prison in 1997, Oliver was hounded out of five towns before giving himself up voluntarily to the police and asking to be housed, eventually in secure accommodation in Milton Keynes at an estimated cost of £5,000 a week. In 1998 Cooke was released after serving nine years of his sixteen-year sentence. He too was subsequently hounded out of one community to another across Britain. A near riot took place outside a police station in Bristol where he was suspected of being held (for his own safety), and while petrol bombs, bottles and bricks were thrown several police officers were injured and a dozen people arrested. Police have revealed that there have been about forty such incidents in various protests around the country, and that most of these have taken place since the introduction of the Sex Offenders Register in September 1997 which, though intended to help statutory agencies to co-ordinate their supervision and monitoring of such offenders, seems to have given the public an expectation that they have a right to know offenders' whereabouts. Local newspapers have been keen to 'name and shame' offenders who are living in their communities by publicizing their addresses, and have thereby fuelled public outrage. In the protest against Cooke in Bristol, which started after a hoax call to the media suggesting that a prisoner covered by a blanket had been taken to the station, several police officers were taken to hospital with cuts and bruises, one had a dislocated shoulder, and another lost several teeth after being hit by a brick.

The public- and the media-driven process of demonizing offenders defines them not only as different from us, but by the same token as 'out there', as essentially strangers. Political and legislative responses have typically focused on the very public face of violence and thereby obscured the overwhelmingly private nature of most forms of violent crime (which in turn are far less likely to be defined as a crime and far less likely to be reported). Any attempts to protect children from the terrible injustice of sexual abuse have to be welcome, but typically the measures proposed and adopted suffer from focusing only on the minority of publicly known, and therefore much more readily visible, targets: that is, those sex offenders who have been convicted. Politicians have scored moral points by the creation of international cross-border regulations to curb child sex tourism involving British citizens in other countries. More recently, the introduction of the Sex Offenders Register has been welcomed by the police, social services and probation officers whose task it is to supervise and monitor the movements of convicted paedophiles released back into the community. Moves to give paedophiles and other sex offenders longer sentences and expanding the legal definition of dangerousness beyond the Mental Health Act are also welcome steps in the overall protection of women and children.[22] A community register is being developed to prevent convicted child sex offenders from loitering around schools and playgrounds.

Yet these strategies, laudable as they may be, are also seriously flawed by the all too familiar process of focusing attention on the few that have been convicted and away from the majority who have not even come under suspicion. The latest community register, banning paedophiles from public places where children might be at risk is a relative red herring, as is the warning to children about talking to and accepting lifts from strangers. The *majority* of paedophiles are not strangers who hang around school playgrounds or public parks waiting to abduct their victims. These public scenarios simply do not reflect the private realities of violence against children. The killing of children following an abduction receives more coverage in the media than any other form of homicide, giving rise to the widespread concern about children's safety from strangers. The facts bear little relation to this perception. Children murdered under the age of sixteen are just like other groups: victims are consistently far more likely to be killed by people known to them. In fact, the number of children to have been killed by strangers has averaged only six or seven per year over the last twenty-five years, making up less than 10 per cent of the total number of children killed each year. The one age group that is consistently at greater risk of being killed than any other, twice as likely as the next highest group (sixteen- to twenty-nine year-olds), is children under the age of one. Once again, overwhelmingly (over 97 percent) they are the victims of people known to them.[23] Similarly, public education posters warning about the dangers of rape emphasize the 'stranger' situation and advise women not to go out late at night and to walk in groups if they do so. Yet, the overwhelming majority of rape and other sexual offences against women occur indoors with men whom they know well. The reality for the majority of women in physically and sexually coercive relationships is that they are far less likely to be attacked when outdoors than in. While men are more likely to be the victims of violence outdoors, women and children are much more likely to be attacked in their own or the offender's homes.[24] Home Office statistics for homicide consistently reveal that the majority of killings are committed by people known to their victims. And while men are roughly three times more likely than women to be killed by a stranger and are at greater risk than females overall, both sexes are most likely to be killed by someone known to them: members of their family, spouses, lovers or friends. Women in particular are most likely to be killed by their spouses or lovers than by anyone else, closely followed by members of their family.[25] The use of surveillance cameras in city centres as a means of detecting and preventing crime is now widespread throughout Britain. It seems quite probable, therefore, that any deterrence of public violence will merely displace it where it cannot be seen on camera: away from men on men, and on to women and children at home.

'They', the violent and sexual offenders, are not usually strangers but integral parts of all of our lives: as fathers, grandfathers, uncles, brothers, boyfriends, teachers, priests, vicars, carers, bosses and neighbours; and sometimes they are even mothers, grandmothers, aunts or sisters as well. They are, in the majority of cases, *known* to their victims, and as such it is the private, hidden violence that occurs in relationships that makes up the overwhelming bulk of violence in society. This is the reality of violent crime. I wonder how many of those who have protested publicly, whether peacefully or in violent vigilante groups, have themselves been victims of other far less visible and unchecked violent perpetrators who are well known to them within their own communities.

We are living within cultural frameworks that predominantly distort and obscure the reality of violence in society. The unquestioned belief in medicine and scientific explanations, allied to a general culture in which genetics and biology are given massive prominence over environmental explanations, all adds up to a society that continues to exist in ignorance and collective denial. Experiences that are in fact widespread are treated as if they are occasional 'freak' occurrences, and the legal and mental health systems actively collude with this particular misconception. Despite professional assurances to the contrary, it is still the case that many family doctors, social workers, psychologists, counsellors and psychiatrists remain ignorant of the links between mental health and violence, and find all manner of other ways of making sense of children's and adults' distress without ever touching upon their experience of violence. Even on the still very rare occasions when abuse, rape or other forms of personal violence are reported, the legal systems that deal with this disclosure are often woefully inadequate and carried out under the suspicious eye of a culture that still doesn't want to believe the victims, or that violence is occurring on the scale that it is.

When it comes to attempting to deal with child abuse and neglect, it is often social workers who are at the cutting edge of child protection. It is true that some have made awful mistakes with fatal consequences, but they are often working within a legal system that hampers their work and with a public that still views them with suspicion, and their profession with derision. Either they are seen as overzealous and interfering, or else – as soon as a child that was known to be at risk is seriously hurt or killed – that they did not do enough. Despite being already overstretched and overburdened by the masses of cases they already have to deal with and further pressure on diminishing resources, it is still widely believed that they are somehow keen to invent abuse out of nothing.

Similarly, the whole endeavour of psychotherapy and coun-selling, one of the few places in society where victims might have the opportunity to reveal their experiences of violence and abuse, has been brought into question in recent years. Since a handful of therapists in North America were accused of brain-washing their clients into believing they were abused when they were not, the entire validity of disclosures of abuse in therapy has been undermined by the 'false memory syndrome'. The out-come of this manoeuvre has not been to protect clients from hordes of so-called seemingly unethical and unscrupulous thera-pists who are obsessed with child abuse, but an attempt to invalidate yet another avenue by which abusers could have their crimes detected, and providing them with yet more means of denying the realities of what they have done. If a handful of psychotherapy clients are supposed to falsely remember that they were abused when they were not, then thousands of abusers could far more readily falsely 'forget' that they have ever abused children. In any case, there is little doubt that it is seen as far worse for a child to falsely accuse an adult of sexual (or other) abuse, than it is for a child who has been abused to have their abuse discredited.

If we just consider the estimated prevalence of the sexual abuse of children in isolation from other forms of maltreatment, then the figures are not only profoundly disturbing but also completely dispel the widespread belief that this form of violence is uncommon. In Britain, the United States, Germany, Switzerland and Australia, prevalence studies consistently find that an estimate of around 10–20 per cent of women and around 8 percent of men experienced sexual abuse as children. In the current population of British children, that would cover 1.5 million girls and half a million boys. Despite the growing mass of evidence indicating the widespread extent of violence against children (and women) in society, the almost knee-jerk response by many to a disclosure of child abuse, rape (or other forms of violence) is still one of disbelief. Victims' disclosures are typically seen as entirely fictional, or that they are massively exaggerating the problem and have misunderstood the situation they were in, or else their motivation for disclosure is questioned by reference to ulterior motives (for example, those seeking compensation for their years of abuse in care are merely claiming they were abused in order to get the money). As much as we may deny the humanity of the perpetrators, we do not collectively wish to hear the accounts of the victims either, especially if they have themselves gone on to offend. It seems that the public in general are only ready to believe in the reality of child abuse and other forms of violence once the myriad of countless moral, social and legal obstacles have been overcome, and a conviction finally reached in the minority of cases that are actually brought to court. The criminal justice system quite simply fails to provide abused children the protection, redress and justice that it is in the unique position of offering.

While there have been painfully slow reforms over recent years that attempt to facilitate the process whereby children can give evidence (such as the use of video link and video tapes), the way in which children are still routinely treated by the courts is itself often abusive and adds immeasurably to what is already an extremely demanding situation. As just one example of this, it is routine in many areas for children to be denied access to therapeutic treatment prior to a court case for fear of their evidence being 'contaminated' by this process. There are often lengthy delays, sometimes well over a year, for a case to reach a hearing, and so the children's ordeal is further prolonged. The Utting report, along with Home Office statistics, have repeatedly shown that the conviction rate for gross indecency with a child under the age of fourteen is just 12 percent. One-third of all children who disclose are under the age of eight, and yet prosecutions are extremely rare in this age group. Similarly, both the NSPCC, child protection agencies and the police broadly agree that at best the conviction rate for child sex offenders represents a mere 10 per cent of the actual sexual offences committed against children. In my experience, the figure is very much lower than this.

It is within a wider culture of disbelief and a professional culture of obfuscation and nativism that those who behave violently – whether towards each other, but especially towards women and children – are permitted to do so with little fear of being discovered. More than this, however, the explanatory frameworks that focus on individuals all serve to obscure from our collective view the fact that many Western societies – including Britain and, increasingly, more globally – have been systematically structured so as to increase the levels of violence within them. By individualizing violence to the extent that is currently the case, whether through the professional processes of medicalization, unquestioned belief in hereditarian and biological explanations, or brutal cultural attitudes of depersonalization and demonization, all of these processes serve to obscure from our collective view the conditions in society that have the potential to inhibit or to encourage violence. As soon as we concentrate our collective attention, millions of pounds of research funds, medical and psychological treatment, public outrage and vilification at or within individuals and their bodies, then we ignore the wider social and economic conditions in which violence takes place and of which it is an integral part. Once we have decided that 'their' biology, 'their' attitudes, 'their' spiritual or moral decrepitude are essentially at fault, then it simply does not matter what sort of world we inhabit or the kind of society we create for ourselves. Brutalizing experiences and conditions that affect large sections of society cease to be relevant in considering the causes of violence, and in thereby influencing our collective responses to it. The contribution of poverty, inequality, discrimination, financial insecurity and other debilitating experiences that are increasingly widespread, and which affect the quality of personal relationships between adults and towards children, are all ignored. If we are to gain a clearer and more humane understanding of why people become violent, then we need to widen our field of view and consider the forms of social ecology that promote violence and in which violence is embedded. Our attention then focuses squarely on the processes of socialization and the conditions under which people are brought up to – and then continue to – express themselves in brutal and destructive ways.

·6·

Violence in Society

It is extremely difficult to estimate the levels of violence in any given society simply because there is such a huge discrepancy between the offences that are recorded and the actual offences committed. In the United Kingdom there are two principal indicators of crime, the official Home Office government-collated *Criminal Statistics England and Wales*, which is based on those 'notifiable' crimes that are reported to the police and recorded by them (whether or not they go to court or lead to a conviction), and the biannual *British Crime Survey*, which relies on interviews with some 15,000 households in the general public about their experiences of crime. Whereas the Home Office statistics cover all of the currently defined forms of crime, the public survey excludes certain offences such as murder, fraud and drug-related crime, and records experiences of violence in more general terms. Given that these measures do not record the same information, there are inevitably discrepancies between the two sets of data. However, the principal reason for the differences lies in the fact that most violence goes unreported. Estimates from the *British Crime Survey* consistently show that the amount of crime actually committed is four times the number of crimes recorded by the police in Home Office statistics. Of all crimes committed, only about half are reported to the police and fewer than a third are recorded.[1]

Some forms of violence are more public and more visible and

it is these forms that make up the bulk of the offences in both of these official estimates of crime rates. Those violent crimes that occur in private are far less likely to be reported either to the police – or anyone else for that matter. The editors of the various *British Crime Surveys* have indeed acknowledged that their estimates of violence cannot be relied upon, particularly as offences between non-strangers will not be mentioned in their interviews; they further estimate that typically only one-fifth of women respondents in the *British Crime Survey* reported domestic assaults upon themselves. Those forms of violence that occur in private in established relationships – so called 'domestic' violence, rape and the abuse of children – are not only less likely to be exposed or reported, but are also less likely to be defined as *crimes* by those involved, whether they are the perpetrators of that violence or their victims. Any official records regarding such invisible offences will therefore be the least reliable of all, and will suffer from the worst problems of underestimation. Returning to the sexual abuse of children as one example of this, as we have seen, the estimates from those organizations involved in child protection are that only 10 per cent of offences ever reach a conviction; it therefore follows that at least a proportion of the remaining nine out of the ten offences remain either actually or statistically concealed. For example, I have known of many sexual offences against teenage (but under-age) children by older men that have gone unrecorded, even when reported by the child's parents, simply because the police would not investigate unless the child themselves made a complaint or statement to them.

Over the course of the last decade in various clinical settings both in the community and in hospital, I have worked with literally hundreds of victims of child abuse and 'domestic' violence, including rape and other forms of sexual coercion and emotional degradation. I can count on the fingers of one hand the number of people for whom the perpetrator of the violence against them has ever been reported to the police, let alone received any form of conviction. For the majority of these people I am the first person whom they have ever told about their experiences, and this is sometimes decades after they have been harmed. In many cases they remain so ashamed of what they have been through, so fearful of the consequences of speaking out and so overwhelmed by the conviction that they were to blame, that it has taken considerable periods of time and the development of trust in the professional relationship before they were able to disclose what they have been through or are still experiencing.

Despite the inherent problems with official information about levels of violence, the data that are available are in their own limited way very informative. If we assume that official figures do indeed represent the tip of the violence iceberg, then whatever is visible does at least offer some useful insights into the nature and composition of the overall iceberg, as well as affording some indication of the levels of violence actually being committed. Violent crime as defined by the Home Office in their annually published *Criminal Statistics England and Wales* is a broad category that includes many forms of crime that are not in fact readily associated with violence at all.[2] These include such crimes as burglary, theft and handling stolen goods, fraud and forgery, or trafficking in drugs. In terms of the forms of interpersonal violence that are the focus of this book, 'Violence against the Person' and 'Sexual Offences' are the two principal categories that are of far greater relevance. 'Violence against the Person' includes many diverse forms of violence such as murder; manslaughter; wounding and assault; infanticide; attempted murder; death by dangerous driving and other motoring offences; child abduction and child abandonment; cruelty to or neglect of children; and also more obscure crimes such as 'procuring illegal abortions', endangering railway passengers (e.g. throwing things at trains), and various ways of 'endangering life at sea'. The other category of violent crime in the Home Office data is that of 'Sexual Offences'. As with 'Violence against the Person', this is quite a broad category which includes within it such diverse offences as buggery; indecent assault on a male or female; rape, unlawful sexual intercourse with a girl ('under thirteen' and 'under sixteen'); incest; abduction; gross indecency with a child; procuration; soliciting; and bigamy. On average, over the last decade less than 1 percent of all notifiable offences were sexual in nature, with such crimes making up less than 15 percent of all of the recorded 'Violent Offences'.[3]

Reviewing the Home Office statistics over the last few decades reveals certain consistent findings regarding the perpetrators of violence, confirming that there is a huge discrepancy between the levels of violence committed by men and women. As an indication of this, in a ten-year period between 1984 and 1994, the number of women found guilty of sexual crimes in all courts represented a mere 1½ per cent of the total of all offenders convicted for these offences. Similarly, in terms of 'Violence against the Person' over the same decade, the number of women found guilty of these offences in all courts totalled less than 9 percent of such convictions.[4] In other words, the majority of violence is committed by men.

Most of that male violence (over 90 per cent of 'Violence against the Person') is considered 'non-life threatening', with 'wounding' easily representing the commonest form. It is not surprising that the most visible forms of violence are the ones that are most notifiable – that is, young men between the ages of sixteen and twenty-four punching, kicking and stabbing each other (as relative strangers) in public places. Despite its reliance on victim-based accounts and its assertions of greater accuracy, the *British Crime Survey* also consistently emphasizes these more public acts of violence, with common assaults making up over two-thirds of all violent crime.[5] Once again, young men under the age of twenty-four are most likely to be both attackers and victims.

In contrast to these generally lesser offences, the most extreme end of violence against the person, the category of homicide (which includes murder, manslaughter and infanticide), is in many ways a more accurate reflection of the nature of violence in general and of concealed violence in particular. Homicide is the one form of violence that is most likely to be both reported and officially recorded simply because it is in most cases so difficult to conceal. In addition, homicide is a relatively clear act in as much as it does not suffer from the same difficulties of definition and interpretation as, say, rape or child abuse. It is for this reason that figures for homicide are widely used as a reliable indicator of levels of violence from which to make comparisons between different countries. As noted in the previous chapter, the homicide statistics reveal that most killings are committed by men known to their victims, and if the victims are women and children, then this is more likely to take place indoors.

One of the most useful aspects of the Home Office figures is that levels of recorded violence can be documented over periods of history and any fluctuations or changes can be monitored. It could be argued that any significant variations in the numbers of notifiable offences do not indicate any changes in the actual number of crimes *committed*, but are the result of changes in the willingness of the public to report such crimes, as well as for the police to take those crimes more seriously. However, since it is clear that the majority of acts of violence continue to go unreported, any significant fluctuations are unlikely to be due to the greater willingness on the part of women and children to do so. The reasons that victims keep quiet have not altered significantly over the last few decades, regardless of the supposedly greater awareness in society about these matters.

Similarly, while it may be true that the police are supposed to have changed their attitude towards 'domestic' violence and child abuse, they cannot record acts that never even reach their attention. In any case, they are generally far too busy to become involved in difficult-to-prove allegations of violence or abuse when pressure is on them to solve much more politically expedient crimes. The police are still reluctant to become involved in many domestic incidents between adults and this in itself is not necessarily a bad thing. There are many occasions when there are no tangible benefits gained from involving the police or the criminal justice system (either for the victim or their assailant) beyond calming a volatile situation down. An arrest or prosecution may not be the most appropriate course of action, nor will it necessarily lead to any cessation of the violence. At times this may even make the whole situation far worse, particularly for the victim for whom it is supposed to offer some protection.

Since official figures reflect a bias towards public acts of violence, any changes in recorded levels will necessarily emphasize changes in these forms. However, this very fact makes the category of 'Violence against the Person' a relatively reliable indicator of overall levels of violence in society for several important reasons. First, since much 'Violence against the Person' is relatively public, these acts will suffer least from the problems of reporting and they are also less likely to suffer from differing recording policies. Secondly, though such a collection of acts are largely made up of violent young men assaulting each other, a significant proportion of these young men will at some stage be involved in other forms of violence. Some young men are only violent while they are young, and sooner or later grow out of this. Others are only ever violent towards other men; some are only violent to their partners; and some only towards children. Some men's violence is specifically sexual, either towards women or towards children. There are, however, a significant proportion of men whose violence is not specific in these ways. There are many men who are violent in different ways and towards a range of victims. It is entirely reasonable to assume therefore that a significant percentage of these men whose acts are recorded are already violent in more concealed ways, or subsequently become violent as they grow older and become part of a domestic set-up. For example, while the peak age for violence against the person is around eighteen, the majority of convictions for sexual offences are for men aged twenty-one and over.

When we examine the changes in the number of recorded offences for 'Violence against the Person' over the last five decades, we discover some extremely disturbing fluctuations. To begin with, the figures reveal that England and Wales have become forty times more violent since the Second World War, an episode that itself did much to elevate the levels of violence throughout Britain (a matter that I shall return to later). Most disturbing of all is that the last decade has seen an increase in the overall numbers as well as a rate of increase in recorded violence on a scale that has previously never been documented. Britain has become much more violent than ever before. Since 1987 there has been a dramatic increase in:

- the total number of recorded violent crimes;
- the rate at which violent crimes are increasing;
- the proportion of all crimes that are violent;
- the proportion of violence that is more serious in nature;
- the number of juveniles who are violent;
- the rate at which the number of violent juveniles is increasing.

The immense scale of this increase is clear when the figures are presented together:

The average increase in total numbers of recorded acts of 'Violence against the Person'[6]

Between 1950 and 1959 it was less than 1,000 per year.
Between 1960 and 1969 it was less than 2,000 per year.
Between 1970 and 1979 it was 6,000 per year.
Between 1970 and 1986 it was 5,000 per year.
Between 1980 and 1986 it was 4,000 per year.

Overall, between 1950 and 1986 it was 3,000 per year.

Between 1987 and 1997 the average rise per year was 12,000.

Therefore it can be seen that the average rise over the last decade has been twice that of any preceding period of time, and four times the average of all the previous years put together. Not only has the rate of increase of violence risen at an alarming rate, but *the increase in the total number of violent crimes against the person over the last decade has far exceeded the total increase over the entire previous thirty-six years.*[7]

The proportion of overall reported crime that is violent is also witnessing a dramatic increase. Yet for the fifth successive year since 1993, the overall levels of reported crime in general have *fallen.* In complete contrast to this general trend, with consistent reductions in virtually all other categories of crime, the number of acts of 'Violence against the Person' and 'Sexual Offences' have continued to rise over the same period of time.[8] Even though the most recent *British Crime Survey* reports that violent crimes have fallen slightly since 1995, the survey still records that overall violent crime has doubled in the last decade.[9]

In addition, the figures demonstrate that the overall profile of violence is itself becoming increasingly brutal. Over the last decade, the proportion of 'Violence against the Person' that is categorized as 'more serious' has increased at a rate unmatched by any other specific category of crime apart from rape. Just as disturbing, the perpetrators of violent acts are also getting progressively younger. In his study of the rise in juvenile violence, Oliver James found that the proportion of crime that is defined as violent committed by ten- to sixteen-year-olds has increased significantly and at an unprecedented rate from 1987 onwards. Just as for the overall figures for 'Violence against the Person', these increases in juvenile violence are in complete contrast to reductions in the overall figures for juvenile crime. So while both the rate and total numbers of all juvenile crime have decreased significantly since 1987, the figures for juvenile 'Violence against the Person' have increased by even greater amounts in the opposite direction.[10] As James points out, all the figures indicate conclusively that the cohort of boys born and raised after 1980 are much more violent than any group born before that day. The infamous actions of Robert Thompson and Jon Venables are therefore part of a wider trend that has seen violent crime more than double as a percentage of all recorded crimes committed by ten- to thirteen-year-olds.[11] None of these increases in levels or rates of violence can be accounted for by changes in population levels since the end of the Second World War. Indeed, the unprecedented increases in 'Violence against the Person' over the last decade are all the more dramatic as the actual numbers of young males have dropped significantly over this period of time.[12]

The fact that we have as a society become more violent, more extremely violent, and that we are producing increasingly younger violent offenders is a reflection of the extent of the degradation in our social ecology. If we are to understand why this is happening we have to look further and further away from the usual focus – i.e. bad or dysfunctional individuals – and broaden our focus of inquiry to take in the changes in society that have occurred over this period of time. We would do far better at furthering our understanding of violence by looking into the conditions that create violence and neglect, than by looking at, or within, those individuals who behave violently. If we are producing increasing numbers of alienated, irresponsible and brutal young men, this is because for many of them society has failed to act responsibly towards them, marginalized them, and has itself become an increasingly brutal place for them to inhabit.

Market forces, violence and the new inequality

At the very beginning of the 1980s, Britain adopted a political system based upon free markets and the international flow of capital was gradually released from any constraints that national borders had hitherto placed in its way. In order for this to happen, individual countries had to embrace the principles of the market and relinquish forms of state intervention and regulation, which in any case would soon become largely irrelevant as the approaching financial waves swept aside all in their wake. The world of unfettered free markets was in the ascendancy and the creation of its global empire was gathering pace. Britain under Mrs Thatcher was one of the first countries to embrace this form of economic organization, and it did so with particular vigour and enthusiasm. The accumulation of wealth and the relentless pursuit of profit was, under Mrs Thatcher's careful husbandry, elevated to the status of a virtue. The ideology of competitive individualism and the relentless pursuit of self-interest and self-reliance became the new philosophy for living. In hindsight, the rising might of the financial world and international capital would have had its way sooner or later regardless of who was in power. It is just that under Mrs Thatcher any pockets of shelter that may have offered people some protection from the hurricane that was coming their way was systematically and swiftly dismantled, leaving many of them utterly defenceless and vulnerable.

The full force of the market would impact in Britain over her decade of power more than in any other developed nation apart from the United States. The United States had already been practising and preaching free market orthodoxy for decades; indeed, North America is both its high priest and its spiritual home. The inevitable social and environmental costs inherent in a system based upon free markets was well known to the preachers of this orthodoxy; it had already given rise to a society characterized by widespread deprivation, extremes of inequality, alienation and, of course, levels of violence. None of this seemed to matter at all. Admittedly the worst aspects of the market would affect those at the bottom of the social heap most; indeed, the market actually depended on large numbers of them being there, so that those at the top had little to lose and everything to gain (or so it seemed to them at the time). Their calculations, however, were purely economic.

The financial world is driven by the pursuit of perpetual growth, a goal that in itself is completely illusory. The overwhelming bulk of international capital has now become totally self-serving. The trillions of dollars, pounds, Deutschmarks and yen that swish around the international superhighway have become virtually devoid of any connection to generating wealth by producing tangible goods and services, but have become a form of legitimized gambling. This is the world of stocks and shares and futures and hedge funds, where men can sit behind computer terminals and buy and sell and speculate to the extent that they can make and lose millions at the flick of a virtual switch. And while these investments and speculations are heaving around the world's main financial centres, they have the power to act as an economic hurricane blowing across continents. The damage they leave in their wake is immeasurable: governments can be toppled and replaced, whole communities can be displaced from their land and their environment be degraded almost overnight; vast tracts of rainforests cleared; whole industries bought, sold or wrecked like children's toys.

As well as the environmental destruction that has taken place, there has also been an unprecedented worldwide degradation of social ecology. Among the many consequences of a world at the mercy of unfettered market forces has been the fragmentation of entire communities and societies and the enormous strain placed upon people's relationships with each other and their children. As Will Hutton put it so succinctly in his critique of market-driven economics and its impact on British society, 'The disintegration of family life and the decline in the public realm that disfigures contemporary Britain may seem far removed from London's financial markets, but they are as linked to them as remote shocks are to the epicentre of an earthquake.'[13]

All forms of violence can and do occur across the whole spectrum of class and income divides, whether it be the maltreatment of children, or one adult abusing another. No section of society is immune from harming, or being harmed by, those around them. Violent people can and do come from all walks of life; however, their numbers are certainly not evenly distributed across class and levels of income. There is a strong connection between levels of violence and levels of income, and yet such a link is obscured both in the popular culture and among the professionals who are paid to deal with the consequences of that violence. The arguments usually go like this. Since violence happens in all classes, including the higher-paid professional and educated groups, then poverty is not related to levels of violence. Conversely, not all people from poor or deprived backgrounds are violent. Such arguments are as erroneous as the ones that refute the links between child abuse and violent adults. Not all men are boxers, but that does not negate the fact that the overwhelming majority of boxers are indeed male. To say that most violent offenders come from deprived homes and are working class, poorly skilled and poorly educated men is not the same as putting it the other way round. The fact remains that the majority of violent people come from the poorest sections of society. The *British Crime Survey* consistently reports that most violence is perpetrated by sixteen- to twenty-nine-year-old men from the lowest social and economic classes in inner cities and their victims are usually from the same groups. Other studies have shown that parents who are on low incomes are far more likely to harm or brutalize their children than parents on high incomes, and that domestic violence is also more likely to occur in low-income, low-status families.[14]

It is the realities of violent homes, child abuse and neglect that leave many victims poorly equipped to deal with life in anything other than destructive ways. The maltreatment of children is where tomorrow's violent adults are created. The equation is in fact quite simple: increase the numbers of people in society who are living in conditions of low income, material deprivation and economic insecurity, and you increase the number of boys who are maltreated and who will sooner or later boost the violence figures as violent men. Then put those same children into continued positions of low income and financial insecurity as potential or actual husbands and fathers, and the cycle of violence continues unhindered. There is inevitably a time delay before those children whose experiences of being raised under the damaging conditions of low income reach the age where they fit the statistics for juvenile and then adult violent crime. The number of children raised after the increase in low-income families in the early 1980s have taken a few years before they have reached the age when they are included in the juvenile (and hence overall) violence statistics.

By any measure, inequalities in Britain are substantially greater than at any time since the Second World War and the numbers of people experiencing relative as well as absolute levels of poverty have soared. Yet the increasing extremes of that inequality have arisen since the early 1980s, and as an inevitable consequence of the free-market revolution. There are several ways of knowing this. First, even though the conditions for attaining both unemployment benefit and income support have become increasingly more stringent, the numbers at this standard of living have ballooned. In 1979 there were 7 million claimants of income support; by 1993 this had risen to 11 million, and yet over the same period of time levels of benefit have become significantly meaner in relation to both average earnings, and even more so when indexed to the cost of living.[15]

Research published by the Joseph Rowntree foundation shows that between 1979 and 1992 the poorest third of the population failed to gain any benefit whatsoever from economic growth. The bottom sixth of the population actually saw their real income fall over this period of time, while the income of the top 10 per cent rose by more than half.[16] The gap between low and high wages is now the highest since records began. The same study shows that the gap between the rich and the poor in this country is now wider than at any point in the last fifty years, and it estimates that one in three children in this country now live in poverty. These conclusions are based in part on the Department of Social Security's report *Households Below Average Income*, which provides a record over time of the differing levels of income across all sections of British society.[17] This report provides a damning picture about the extent of the inequalities in Britain today as well as the shifting patterns since 1979 when the wholescale adoption of free-market policies began in earnest. In 1979 only 9 percent of children lived in households with less than *half* the average income, but by 1996 this had increased to 31 percent. Taking half the average income as a reasonable baseline measure of poverty, by 1996 nearly a third of all children – 3.9 million – lived in households with less than this amount. According to the survey, children's 'income' position (amount of disposal income per child within a given family unit) has been dramatically affected by increased unemployment and the rise in lone parenthood; since there has been a substantial increase in both single parents and couples not in full-time employment, the representation of children in the lower-income groups has also increased significantly.

A report published in 1998 by the United Nations Development Programme includes an index for poverty in the world's richest countries.[18] This index gives a measure of the percentage of the population in a country that does not reach a basic level of income, literacy and health care. According to this index, Sweden comes out with the least percentage disadvantaged at just 6.8 percent, whereas the United Kingdom comes out as one of the worst (at 15 percent), closely followed by the United States, which is the worst of all at 16.8 percent. Thus the United States is the richest country in the world, and also the most unequal society in the developed world. As well as being the most unequal society in the industrialized world, the United States is also the most violent – and this is not a coincidence. The States has much higher homicide levels than those found in comparable European countries and in Japan, and in some cases as much as ten times the rate found in these countries. Well over a decade ago, the American criminologist Elliott Currie, commenting on the high levels of violent crime in the United States compared with other rich nations, wrote that:

> It isn't accidental that among the developed countries, the United States is afflicted simultaneously with the worst rates of violent crime, the widest spread of income inequality, and the most severe public policies towards the disadvantaged. The industrial societies that have escaped our extremes of criminal violence tend either to have highly developed public sectors with fairly generous systems of income support, relatively well developed employment policies, and other buffers against the 'forces of the market', or (like Japan) to accomplish much the same ends through private institutions backed by an ethos of social obligation and mutual responsibility. By any measures we can construct, these countries have been less plagued by the extremes of inequality and economic insecurity. Our pattern of development into an advanced industrial nation on the other hand, has been unusually harsh and disruptive of the conditions that inhibit interpersonal violence.[19]

Currie argued that the levels of violence in the United States were due to the greater levels of inequality as a consequence of both employment practices and meaner welfare provision. The States also has all the worst conditions for violence to be encouraged – the widest spread of income inequality, the least public policies towards its disadvantaged in terms of welfare and health care provision, and the worst employment policies. More than in any country since the Second World War, the quantity and quality of employment in the States has been left up to the market to determine. Not only have unemployment rates in the States been much higher than in other countries, but at the same time there was less spent on health and welfare provision than in comparable countries; and it seems certain that the higher levels of violence have reflected this. The same correlation between employment, welfare and violence was evident when different American states were compared with each other. Currie carried out comparisons between Texas, where welfare payments in 1980 were some of the lowest in the United States, with Wisconsin, whose citizens at that time were more protected from the effects of market-driven inequality than in any other state. Texas had the same number of families receiving benefit despite having three times the population of Wisconsin and five times its number of poor people. The homicide rate in Texas was six times that of Wisconsin.

Global comparisons of violence between countries have tended to rely on homicide rates as a measure of levels of violence. They have found that in general terms the richer (economically developed) countries suffer less in terms of violence than the poorer countries. Yet the levels of violence do not simply equate with the wealth of a nation, for some poorer countries are not as violent as they should be, while other richer nations, such as the United States, are much more violent than this relationship would predict. If, however, the definitions of violence are broadened to include military conflict and civil unrest, then the relationship between absolute levels of poverty and absolute levels of violence become clearer. Absolute levels of poverty is to violence what dry grass is to bush fire. Political stability is largely dependent on economic stability and so the poorer a country, or the more deprived large sections of its membership are, the greater the likelihood of wholescale violent unrest. This is all the more so if a disadvantaged section in a country feels marginalized or excluded from political activity. Of the ten most in-debt countries, eight have suffered civil war or violent conflict since 1990. Of the twenty-five most in-debt countries, fifteen are currently countries with conflict. Importantly, military conflict or civil unrest are not in any way disconnected from the other forms of interpersonal violence that have so far been concentrated on in these pages. Put men in brutal conditions and they will behave brutally; expose them to that brutality for long enough and they will not stop behaving aggressively once they are out of the original situation.

The immense scale of the two world wars fought this century, which involved such large numbers of the male population, saw many men returning deeply traumatized and altered by their experience of conflict, carnage or imprisonment. That a significant number of these men returned home to be violent, over-controlling and autocratic has been a largely hidden cost of the wars, once again absorbed within families and concealed behind closed doors. Unless they were so traumatized that they were unable to function, most of these men rarely sought, nor were they given, professional help. It has been argued that their experiences at war have left shock waves of violence through society which have been transmitted across subsequent generations, many of whom had not even experienced the wars directly.[20]

Once the definitions of violence are narrowed down to exclude military conflict, acts of terrorism or civil unrest, as Currie and others have done, the degree of violence seems not to be directly related to the overall wealth of the country, but the extent of the inequality in it. The greater the degree of inequality in terms of employment practices and hence income levels, and the lower the welfare provision in terms of its proportion of GNP, then the higher the rates of violence.[21] This has generally led to the conclusion that it is *relative* levels of income within a country, rather than *absolute* poverty, that determines the levels of violence. Since it is argued that absolute poverty only applies to people in the poorest of nations, anyone living in, say, Britain or the United States could, by these standards, only be seen as being relatively poor. However, the United States has become so polarized along economic and racial lines that, according to United Nations definitions, there are sections and communities within it that are so deprived that they would in fact qualify for 'Third World' status. In some ways being poor in a richer country is worse than being poor in a 'developing' one. At least in poorer countries the predicament is one that affects the majority of people, which nurtures traditional forms of community and solidarity. Being poor when many around you are not breeds alienation and resentment. Currie argues that economic development closely allied to market principles undermines the forms of collective solidarity so often evident in many of the poorest nations:

Economic development within the market system tends to undermine traditional institutions of support and mutual obligation; what is most crucial in influencing the pattern of violence and crime is the extent to which these traditional support mechanisms manage to survive in the face of that disruption (recall Japan's private mechanisms of social obligation) or are supplanted by new ones (Western Europe's welfare state). Where this happens the overall effect is to decrease interpersonal violence over time. Where it fails to happen, economic growth may weaken or destroy the supportive relations that existed in more traditional communities without putting anything substantial in their place. The result is an impoverished rural and urban underclass deprived of respectable livelihoods, torn away from personal attachments and informal control, and dependent on an often inadequate labour market as the exclusive provider of social integration, material welfare and self-esteem.[22]

Currie identifies that it is market-driven employment practices that are central to the creation of wide disparities of income as well as undermining processes of social integration and social obligation. Market forces and the global flow of capital have directly affected employment practices more than any other aspect of life, both in Britain and elsewhere. Until recent decades, the generation of wealth used to be based on actual material goods in manufacturing, industry, farming and natural resources. All of these provided employment for people in one way or another and, until relatively recently, depended on a largely formal male workforce who could in turn provide for their families. This in turn enabled an informal female workforce, who though they received no official salary, nonetheless took care of all the work within the home, and who were largely responsible for the task of child-rearing. This is no longer the case. In a world in which the financial sector takes precedence over all other forms of income generation, and in the absence of employment targets and policies, the quality and quantity of employment is left to the whims of the market. A society run along the lines of unrestricted free market economies requires fundamental changes in the way people work. The fundamental changes that have occurred in the labour market have generated both high levels of unemployment as well as profoundly altering the nature and quality of whatever work is available. In addition to increased numbers of families claiming state benefit, many who exist above this level do so not only on low income, but on an insecure income. As well as high levels of people out of work, market forces and the deregulation of employment have also led to huge increases in poorly paid, part-time or temporary jobs. This in turn has led to widespread financial insecurity, which affects most people who are in work as well as those who depend upon them. The ramifications of this inequality and instability for the social and material conditions of many people's lives has been catastrophic, tearing apart both families and communities. The social cost of market reforms has been people's health, their relationships with each other and with their children, and ultimately in terms of the dramatic increases in levels of violence in society. All of this, of course, has enormous implications for public spending in terms of welfare, social and health services and a rising prison population.

The greatest disparities in income, the worst levels of deprivation and the most extreme social consequences are closely linked to sharp rises in both unemployment and poorly paid work. Official figures underestimate the actual numbers of adults who are out of work simply because they are based solely on those claiming unemployment benefit. There are many more outside of the current narrow definitions who are definitely not 'job-seekers'. These include those who are no longer seeking work either because they are too sick, because there is no work for them to look for, or because any work they might do would bring in less than their income support. It is estimated that altogether about a third of the adult working population are either officially unemployed or economically inactive and it is mainly men that make up the bulk of this problem: some 4 million of them who are in one way or another out of work.[23] By the spring of 1996, a fifth of all households containing members of working age had no adult in work in Britain compared with under one in ten in 1979. By the same year, almost

25 percent of people in the poorest fifth of the income distribution in this country lived in unemployed families compared with only 10 per cent in 1979.[24] High levels of unemployment have hit young, unskilled men the hardest as the demand for their labour has fallen dramatically, as has the extent of their earning potential and their prospects of meaningful work.

This growing section of society who are living in poverty have borne the brunt of market force reforms. Indeed, violence is such an integral part of life in the poorest sections of society that it can no longer even be considered as beyond the norm, or as deviant or pathological. The most recent *British Crime Survey* found that as many as a fifth of young men under the age of twenty-four suffered a violent attack between 1995 and 1997.[25] Separate Home Office studies reveal that relationships in as many as one in four households involve domestic violence, overwhelmingly from men to women.[26] Poverty, deprivation and neglect go hand in hand with the maltreatment of children. The experience of powerlessness and exploitation that is child abuse is an integral part of the experience of powerlessness and marginalization of large sections of society. Deliberate policies based upon inequality and economic insecurity profoundly increase the conditions in which the maltreatment of children is likely to occur, and their development into adults with violent personalities, as well as pushing those with already limited means of coping beyond their ability to do so.

Poverty is not merely an abstract concept or a statistical quirk. Poverty and deprivation have a constant and relentless impact on people's lives. We don't like to imagine that there are families in Britain in the late twentieth century who are struggling to feed their children or to remain warm. Families that have to make choices about what food to buy and about what not to buy in order to pay for other basic necessities such as heating or electricity. In a market force economy that emphasizes the supremacy of individual freedom of choice, that choice has become increasingly dependent on the size of one's income. Poverty severely restricts choices about what to eat, where to shop, what to wear, where to live, or the ability to holiday and to get away from everyday routine. Those who live in the poorest sections of society experience greater levels of stress, impoverished physical health, and significantly shorter life expectancy.[27] The connection between low income and the experience of personal distress such as depression is one of the most consistent findings in the mental health literature over many years.[28] Poverty and its associated social and health-related problems undermine educational achievement and stifle educational aspirations. As well as being associated with poorer health, limited education, inadequate or insufficient food and being cold in winter, poverty is also about shelter. At one and the same time as the numbers of people on low income have burgeoned, state benefits and housing provision have been reduced as a deliberate policy to minimize welfare spending. The housing policies of the 1980s systematically moved away from cheap housing provision by councils to private ownership or private renting. This has had a dramatic effect on the quantity and quality of homes for people on low incomes. Indeed, the full extent of poverty in Britain has been underestimated by the *Households Below Average Income* statistics: excluded from their figures are those living in residential institutions (including those with long-term mental health problems and the prison population) and the homeless, whether they are living in 'Bed and Breakfast' type accommodation or sleeping rough on the streets.

The number of homeless people has increased every year since 1979, many of them being adults with children. In 1994 there were an estimated 200,000 homeless, three times as many as in 1979. Financial constraints on local authorities has meant that any spending on the few houses left outside of private ownership has not been well maintained. Those poorest sections of the community in council-run estates have drifted into overcrowded, cramped living conditions with little or no privacy. This has in turn intensified the breakdown of urban life, as the most troubled and troublesome communities have been herded into increasingly American-style ghettos – with some being segregated along racial lines as well. We have become not only economically polarized, but geographically polarized as well. Every area of the country has become divided into the more expensive and more exclusive areas, with better schools, better facilities and better health provision, while the areas most in need of support have been left to become rundown concentrations of social disharmony, violence and crime. These are everyday realities in the United Kingdom in the late twentieth century when they should be conditions that passed away in the nineteenth century. The United Kingdom may be considerably richer as a nation than at any time in her history, but not all of her citizens are able to benefit from this.

Nowhere is the relationship between economic deprivation and violence clearer than for those children at the very bottom of the social heap who are removed from home and put into 'care' or put on the 'at risk' register. For example, parents of neglected 'failure to thrive' children are almost universally characterized by low income and material deprivation. You will hardly ever hear of a child from a middle-class family 'failing to thrive' or being brought to the attention of child protection professionals, and this is not simply because maltreatment in middle-class and more educated families is far less likely to be detected. Not only is child maltreatment more likely in low-income families, but the nature of that child maltreatment, as well as its severity, also changes as we move up and down income levels. Children of chaos, as defined earlier, are almost invariably from the poorest homes. Children from the poorest backgrounds are also much more likely to be neglected and to experience physical abuse, whereas those from wealthier homes tend to be controlled or manipulated through emotional means. There is no doubt that access to money can reduce the risk to children, no matter how disharmonious the household may be. Parents with money can employ other people to look after their children, go on holiday, and live in more spacious housing in better, less crime-afflicted areas. Although childhood sexual abuse cuts across income levels to a greater degree than any other form of child maltreatment, in my own experience it is again more likely, more severe, more uninhibited and more prolonged in homes with relatively lower incomes.

As well as having a direct impact in terms of the material conditions of people's lives, there are also indirect social consequences of being unemployed, as well as growing up in an unemployed family, especially over long periods of time. Work confers a sense of place in a hierarchy of social relations, both within the immediate organization of employment and beyond it. Those who work belong, those who are out of work are excluded. Work gives shape to people's lives; as with all other purposeful human activity, it is imbued with meaning and significance that extends far beyond the wage packet. Unemployment not only brings a loss of status and value, but also alienation, hopelessness and despair. Many of the men in this position, especially the unskilled, can expect little other than to work for very low wages or to live off income support and the black economy. Research has demonstrated 'the significantly raised mortality of the unemployed in comparison to all men of working age' as well as double the incidence of mental health problems.[29] In his analysis of the growing inequalities in Britain in the 1980s, Richard Wilkinson found that as the inequalities widened, so self-esteem among the poor fell. This translated into reductions in life expectancy as a result of both the psychological stresses of poverty and its impact on deteriorations in health. He found that suicide rates for young men aged between fifteen and twenty-four rose sharply as their relative earnings deteriorated, employment prospects fell sharply, and benefit entitlement was reduced.[30] By 1998 the second biggest killer of men in Britain under the age of thirty-five was suicide.

The quality and permanence of jobs available to young men has decreased markedly, as have the conditions of work that might be available to them. Not only do many find themselves on the outside of employment, but many stand on the fringes of whatever low pay and temporary work is within their reach. The only purchase that they have with which to gain access to employment also discriminates against them. Where there has been some growth in employment opportunities, this has been in part-time work and in the service industries, both of which have offered greater opportunities for women rather than men. While male unemployment has risen since 1979, female employment has actually increased.[31] Over half of the recent growth in employment (spring 1993 to spring 1996) has been in part-time employment, and the majority of part-time employees are women. However, many of these jobs offer no formal employment protection, are only on a temporary basis, and the majority are poorly paid.[32] On their own, such jobs offer insufficient income to support a family.

The psychological effects of unemployment have a far greater impact on men, particularly young and unskilled working-class men who have traditionally defined themselves and have been defined by society through their work. Despite the increasing presence of women in employment, their self-esteem is still not as dependent on being in work as it is for, especially, working-class men. Women are still able to define themselves through their social relationships and their associations to a far greater extent than men can. If they are not working, then their existence as mothers, daughters or wives continues to hold, regardless of their employment status. However, women and children are affected by these large numbers of economically inactive men either because they are dependent on them and therefore share the same poor standard of living, or else because they bear the brunt of their frustration and their despair. Between 1979 and 1995 the number of children living in families without a full-time worker has increased from 18 percent to 31 percent.[33] The links between unemployment, poverty and violence are unequivocal: NSPCC surveys have consistently found that almost two-thirds of the fathers of children who have been placed on the 'at risk' register were not in full-time employment and that violent partners had much higher than average levels of unemployment.[34] These findings have been consistently demonstrated in other studies.[35]

Those who are out of work are alienated both through their direct exclusion from mainstream society and their inability to operate in a world in which people's sense of self-worth has become increasingly defined by material possessions and rates of consumption. The capacity to be part of the wider community, to be a 'consumer', depends upon spending power. All of this has created an underclass of marginalized, excluded and hence alienated young men for whom violence has become an integral part of survival and a necessary way of life – no longer the 'have nots', but the 'have nothings'. The impact of very low income and the deprivation this brings is relentless and destructive. For many of those who live under the pressure of being at the bottom of the social heap, relationships are frequently characterized by violence. Indeed, there is a sense whereby these men and boys need to operate aggressively in order to survive, and reduced to the physicality of their bodies their only means of feeling in control is to express themselves through physical, and frequently brutal, means. Such exclusion necessarily impacts upon those groups in society that are marginalized or discriminated against in other ways, and it is no surprise therefore to find that poor, young, dark-skinned men feel most alienated, and thereby over-represented, in the violence figures. There has been a well-publicized increase in gang culture as a feature of alienation among the young, invariably from the poorest sections of society. The association with gangs and a marginalized subculture confers a desperately needed form of belonging and collective power among the most alienated and, usually, poorly socialized young. In some cases this has led to expressions of collective physical and sexual violence that for many of those involved might not have emerged had they been on their own.

It is under these harsh, ruthless and competitive conditions that working-class, male identities are shifting and becoming distorted. Violence is also about the distorted definitions of masculinity in Western cultures, cultures where young men not only feel profoundly alienated from their society, but also where they are brought up to consider it 'natural' to express themselves through physical and often brutal means. It is not just poverty alone that can account for extremes of violence; we also have to consider the gendered nature of what is predominantly a male problem and the way both economic and cultural deprivation interact. It is not only the direct effect of market forces on the material conditions of people's lives that hardens attitudes and impoverishes the ways in which we treat each other, but a highly commercialized environment also distorts our cultural frameworks in much more subtle and insidious ways. Nowhere is this distortion more blatant than the way in which sexuality and sexual relationships have become commercially defined. Sex has become not only an advertising tool used to sell a limitless array of products, but has itself become a commodity like any other in the market place. Our collective frameworks for making sense of our relationships with one another, and for understanding sex in particular, have become so intimately bound up with blatant commercial interest and exploitation that it is almost impossible to separate fact from fiction. Depictions of women in pornographic magazines and films as impersonal sexual objects desperately seeking gratification promotes a similarly 'dissociated' version of male sexuality. The concept of impersonal sex, sex without risk, sex without responsibility, and sex devoid of any meaningful relationship, has reduced it to the level of any other commercially available leisure activity. The discrepancies between marketed sex in all its objectified forms and the subtle realities of personal relationships serve only to confuse and mystify, leaving adults, let alone young people and children, unable to know what to expect from their intimate relations. Confusing and commercially manipulated frameworks about sexuality create an environment in which young people are unable to make sense of their experiences, and within the void between that experience and their limited understanding they can be readily exploited, deceived, raped and abused.

The impersonal way in which sex is presented to young people also leads to horribly distorted expressions of male sexuality, which encourages young men to treat members of the opposite sex with a detached indifference, thereby increasing the chances of males behaving brutally and of harm being done. The ultimate icon of British masculinity has for decades been James Bond, upper class, highly intelligent and refined, a perfect representative of the British empire. All of this is juxtaposed with emotionally detached killer as well as callous lover, unfailingly able to perform both of these functions in and out of bed as he hops effortlessly from one beautiful foreign women to another. It is interesting to note that the very qualities of complete emotional detachment and charm that makes James Bond such a universally appealing male role model are the same characteristics that are supposed to define the psychopath.

The changing face of work

The changes in the labour market have adversely affected all but the very wealthiest sections of society. Those who have been fortunate enough to find employment have been affected just as much by the changes that have taken place, even though their standard of living may not be as deprived as those who have been marginalized nor their rates of violence as high. There are many people in employment, even at relatively much higher income levels, who are precariously hanging on to their standard of living and who are experiencing increasingly brutal conditions at work. The deregulation of employment practices since the early 1980s has been relentless and thorough. This has served to shift the balance of power in favour of employers to such an extent that many employees have little or no protection or rights. Among the many reforms have been the systematic reduction in the power of the trade unions, the abolition of the wages councils, and the wholescale 'casualization' and deregulation of employment. Thus we now have no regulation of working hours, Sunday and holiday trading, no legal protection or benefits such as sick pay or holiday entitlement for those in work under temporary contracts, no minimum wage legislation, and no right to representation in the workplace. By 1994 Britain had the least protected workforce in the industrialized world apart from North America.[36]

Many of these changes have been championed as offering both employees and consumers greater freedom of choice, especially the casualization of work into part-time and temporary work and the extension of working times and hours. However, this new flexibility has not been in the interests of many employees or their families, but is essentially for the benefit of the biggest companies with the largest number of employees. Two part-time workers can produce the same as one full-time equivalent, but at a fraction of the overheads, and casual workers can be hired or fired as demand rises and falls. As Will Hutton points out, a deregulated and flexible labour market means that employers and companies can displace all of the risks inherent in the free market on to their workforce, thereby letting their employees and their families suffer the consequences of any fluctuations in the economy or in demand. Without any legislation or protection, employees are reduced to mere disposal commodities, as easily exploitable replaceable units.

In 1975, 55 percent of the adult population held full-time tenured jobs, but in 1993 the proportion had dropped to a mere 35 percent. It is mainly men who have directly suffered as a result of this, as full-time employment for men has plummeted by 20 per cent since 1977.[37] The concept of a 'job for life' no longer exists and the full-time, permanent contract allied to the forty-hour week is rapidly disappearing. The pattern of employment has increasingly become one of periods of employment interspersed with periods of unemployment, or moving from one temporary job to another. Even many of those with permanent jobs are also faced with the ever-present threat of redundancy. In the wake of market forces, whole industries can be 'downsized' or shut down, thereby removing almost overnight the effective employment of entire communities. Companies can at a whim withdraw their capital, but their employees no longer even have the legal right to withdraw their labour.

The threat of redundancy coupled with the reality of periods of low income and economic inactivity is now a daily reality for literally millions of the working population whose lives have thereby become characterized by financial insecurity. There is a sense in which predictability and security of income are just as important as its absolute level: along with the growing inequality of the 1980s and 1990s has been a huge rise in economic insecurity. The material foundation upon which we build our lives depends to a large extent on predictability and safety of income, without which we suffer a profound loss of control over our lives. For example, it makes it very hard to take on a mortgage or maintain payments or to plan for the future in private or occupational pension schemes. Prolonged exposure to uncertainty and threat is just as bad for adults as it is for children.

A market-driven economy requires large numbers of people to be out of work in order to cut down on overheads as well as to drive down wages. The existence of so many people out of work, whether temporarily or permanently, creates an atmosphere of fear and hence a readily malleable and exploitable workforce. Those in employment are required to work harder for less pay and in more demanding and insecure conditions. Already unprotected, those who are in employment feel privileged to be exploited because they know that if they do not like it they are easily replaced by the many waiting eagerly in the wings to take up any vacancies that might arise. Conditions of employment across all income levels have become so brutal, dehumanizing and impersonal that in many cases it is no exaggeration to conceive of the workplace as the human equivalent of the battery farms in which chickens are kept to achieve maximum output at minimum cost.

In the private sector and the privatized national industries and utilities, profit margins have been boosted by massive job cuts. The relentless need to generate dividends for shareholders has led to efficiency measures involving severe job losses, leaving the remaining workforce not only insecure, but also having to do the same amount of work with less staff. Where profits have reached a plateau, the same process of wholescale job losses have occurred as already large companies have merged into even larger ones, shedding huge swathes of their workforce to create efficiency savings and boost shareholder dividends and share prices. We have got so used to these large numbers of job losses that euphemisms such as 'downsizing' 'rationalization', 'efficiency measures' and 'restructuring' have become part of everyday language. It is strange how those who argue against a minimum wage insist that such legislation would lead to job losses, when all that has happened for nearly two decades of unfettered market forces is exactly that. The culture of business and the spirit of entrepreneurialism under Mrs Thatcher encouraged millions to unrealistically set up their own businesses and thereby to become self-employed. Many of these smaller companies were much less able to withstand any fluctuations in the economy, leaving these people and their employees out of work. Many of those who have managed to hang on to their businesses have found that they need to work tirelessly just to survive.

In the public sector, efficiency gains and increases in performance have not been achieved through employing more staff, but by requiring the existing workforce to work excessively hard and for longer hours. While the population as a whole has become older, sicker and beset with more social problems, those whose responsibility it is to meet these demands have done so with no extra resources or staff. Shorter hospital waiting times, larger class sizes, the protection of greater numbers of 'at risk' children or the maintenance of an increasing prison population have all been achieved at great personal cost to employees and their families. While the efficiency reforms in the public sector were supposed to trim off the excess fat, what has in fact happened has reduced resources to the bone marrow. These unreasonable demands have led to widescale low morale, and epidemic levels of ill health and stress among those in the workforce. The Nuffield Trust, an independent health study unit, brought together the findings from several hundred previous studies to provide the most comprehensive analysis of sickness in NHS employees.[38] They found consistent patterns of relatively high rates of ill health among NHS employees, including levels of psychological disturbance ranging from anxiety to chronic depression. These forms of personal distress were experienced by as many as half of all those in various different professions including nurses, doctors and managers. Right across the public sector, the picture of overwork has been the same: greater demands, less staff, longer working hours. Many are moving into the private sector, leaving altogether, or drifting wearily towards early retirement. There are serious problems in the recruitment of nurses, doctors and teachers, and this is not simply because many of them feel poorly remunerated for the work that they do or overburdened by the demands placed upon them. Doctors, senior nurses, senior members of the police, headteachers, prison governors and their counterparts in other public services are all telling of the same problems of overwork and low staff morale.

The state of staff morale is not just related to pay and the quantity of the work, but also what has happened to its *quality*. Many employees across different professions in the public sector feel deeply disillusioned with the changes to the nature and aims of the work that they are required to do. The constant reforms they have been asked to implement over the last decade have not been shaped by their professional expertise nor by client need, but instead have been driven by political dogma and based almost solely on economic imperatives. This has left a 'credibility vacuum' between what they know they should be doing and what their work has been reduced to. The managerial ethos of business has applied hard economics to patients, pupils, students and other 'customers' of public services. In a form of Orwellian doublespeak, whenever the word 'quality' has been used it has actually meant 'quantity'. Shorter waiting times to access fewer hospitals that are manned by fewer staff, and in which patients spend less time recovering, can only lead to a better quality of service by defying the laws of mathematics. Only based on the same twisted logic could the conclusion be reached that the ratio of children to teachers did not matter, that class size was irrelevant to the quality of children's education.

The fact that most adults and young people in Britain who are eligible to work are either out of work, living on poverty-level incomes or in conditions of permanent stress and insecurity has had dreadful effects on the wider society. And, as we have seen, even many of those in work live in a state of financial insecurity. All of this brings with it difficulties not only in terms of economic survival, but inevitably it has placed an unsustainable strain on relationships both at work and in people's personal lives. The consequences of this in terms of our social ecology has been catastrophic: for relationships, for families, and for children in particular. The hours of work needed to earn decent wages continue to increase, and at the same time working long or unsociable hours to support a family impoverishes family life. Many parents both need to work as a matter of economic necessity rather than choice. Those who are working, and who can afford it, sub-contract the rearing of their children to others, while those who cannot afford to do this either have to rely heavily on their families or else leave their children unsupervised for long periods of time. It has become harder and harder for men and women in these circumstances to hold on to their marriages or relationships, let alone to parent their children adequately.

Compared with the rest of Europe, Britain has one of the lowest life expectancy rates, the most deregulated labour markets, the longest working hours, *and* the highest divorce rate – as well as the highest proportion of single-parent families. In 1998 in Britain a quarter of all families were headed by lone parents, whose numbers have more than doubled since 1979 – representing an increase of over 1½ million more single parents since that time. Many of these (mainly single mothers) are living in extreme poverty, with over half of them in the lowest income bracket.[39] Without men to provide for them and their children, these single mothers have drifted into poverty. Given that most part-time work is poorly paid, this is simply not an option for many of them: either because the hours are totally incompatible with child care (most part-time work does not fit conveniently around school hours) or because the work is so poorly paid that there is no financial gain in wages over benefit payments. Their experience of poverty is of course also associated with the experience of ill health, stress and violence. Even given its limitations, the most recent *British Crime Survey* found that after young men, the next highest risk group were young women and single parents, one in ten of whom said that they had experienced some form of assault.

Most mothers can understand how a very tired woman could shake, or even attack, their incessantly crying newly born child in frustration and despair. Add the pressure-cooker atmosphere of poverty, deprivation and isolation, put the people concerned in violent relationships and give them a history of their own childhood abuse out of which they have only recently emerged, and it is not difficult to understand why some women lose control completely. Put women under severe enough conditions of powerlessness and they too will behave violently: the only form of violence where women approach male levels is towards very small children. It is still predominantly women who look after young children and especially babies; women's levels of infanticide, the killing of children under the age of one, is the only form of violence that exceeds that of men.

For an increasing number of children the world into which they are born is a harsh, uncaring and often violent one. Households in which the relationships are characterized by tension, discord, aggression or fragmentation are dramatically on the increase, and without doubt this is having profound consequences for the children who are caught up in this. Many adults who are looking after children, even if they do not mistreat them in the ways that have been so much the focus of this book, are themselves becoming weary, unwell, distressed or, at the very least, intolerant and irritable. The changing face of work has led to widespread stress and illness, some of which is expressing itself in the form of child abuse and domestic violence. For those adults looking after children who are not experiencing the extremes of poverty and neglect, the demands of economic survival and uncertainty can still be expressed in a kind of tired neglect of parental care and familial time. Their attitude towards their children is a sort of mild resentment, seeing them as yet another demand upon their already drained energy and resources. Many parents who are trying their utmost, and with the best will in the world, still end up harming each other and their children in the face of brutal work conditions and financial insecurity, a predicament over which they have little or no control. The conditions under which children have the opportunity to develop within a relatively benign and stable world, or to receive the patient and unpressured attention from adults around them, are becoming harder to find and the preserve of fewer and more privileged people. For the most marginalized sections of society, this has led to levels of violence and numbers of violent juveniles on a scale that has never been seen before.

As well as the dramatic increases in the numbers of violent juveniles, another way in which this trend is revealing itself is the number of children who are being excluded from school on account of their disruptive, unmanageable or violent behaviour. A recent Children's Society report found that between 1990 and 1996 there was a 460 *per cent* increase in permanent exclusions of children from primary and secondary schools in England and Wales, some involving children as young as four years old.[40] As a measure of how divided and polarized a society Britain has become, the report shows how some deprived areas were twenty times more likely to exclude children than others, and that African-Caribbean boys were estimated to be five times more likely than white pupils to be excluded. These children's limited educational possibilities will in turn make them less employable in an already ruthless job market. As increasing numbers of children develop distressed, troubled and also violent ways of expressing themselves in response to the unfavourable conditions in which they are raised, so the collective response has been, predictably, to explain their difficult behaviour in terms of their faulty biology.[41]

The global market, cultural frameworks and personal responsibility

While the impact of market forces on the social and economic fabric of British life has been profound, the experience in this tiny island is but one piece of a much larger jigsaw. The extent of the catastrophe that is unfettered market forces cannot be fully appreciated on a national level alone. It is only when one extends the view to encompass the global scale of this man-made disaster can we really appreciate more clearly how such economics operate and the consequences for our worldwide social ecology. The global picture is also one of inequalities and of a widening gap between rich and poor. While there are differences in standards of living and health between rich and poor within the richest nations, this pales into insignificance when we examine the discrepancies between those rich countries and the poorest ones. The discrepancies in life expectancy between those living in the richest and poorest countries continues to broaden to a point that is rapidly approaching double.[42] That this gap exists to the degree that it does is an obscenity, but the fact that it is increasing is a direct function of many immoral economic and political policies. It is not malnutrition, drought, famines, civil wars, military conflict or even disease that is the biggest killer of people in the world today. Even the World Health Organization finally acknowledged in its annual report that most deaths in the world are caused by *poverty*.[43] This poverty is neither inevitable nor necessary, but is a function of a system that has been structured so as to enhance the wealth of a tiny minority – most of whom reside in the richest countries. Indeed, the standard of living in the richer nations depends entirely on the existence of poverty and the exploitation of the poorest nations, where it occurs overseas and out of sight. While billions are spent in the West on expensive and sophisticated treatments for cancer and heart disease, millions die of economic and political neglect in the poorer world for want of a basic standard of living. Despite the fact that there is more than enough food available to feed the entire human population, millions are still left to die as the distribution of resources continues to become the preserve of a relatively tiny minority.[44] Few have written as cogently about world hunger and poverty as Susan George. In her analysis of the economics behind this global catastrophe she writes:

> The present world capitalist order sanctions private ownership while taking no responsibility for those who own nothing. It has been incapable of setting upper limits for accumulation of riches by an individual, a corporation or, for that matter, a nation. By contrast, the lower limit – death by hunger – is very clearly defined. For a world economy ruled by competition and the profit motive, millions of people are utterly useless ... World capitalism would prefer that such 'useless' people disappear – at present, starvation is one avenue towards this end.[45]

The globalization of the market has not just led to unimaginable inequalities in material conditions at national and global levels, it is also distorting the political and ideological landscape of our lives. The politics of the market is shaping our cultural frameworks and redefining not only how we see and feel about each other, but also how we see our relationship with our society and ultimately our world. National governments are becoming less relevant in this new world order and, as their power diminishes, so too does the political influence of ordinary people.

We become politically disenfranchised. As elected governments come to matter less and less, so market-based capitalism seriously undermines any notion of democracy and the political influence of ordinary people. The major players are the powerful banking and financial institutions of the richer nations, among them the World Bank and the International Monetary Fund, as well as the increasingly powerful multinational companies such as the arms, petroleum and chemical industries. Political decisions are reduced to economic imperatives and the social or environmental impact of those decisions is quite literally immaterial.[46]

The movement of political parties and Western governments towards a central position in which there are no fundamental challenges to free market economics is a measure of how successful and how powerful this unrestricted form of capitalism has become. It is ironic that while the market promises increased choice, our political options have become narrowed and limited. We may now be able to alter the tone and volume of our political lives, but we are no longer able to change the programme. Any articulation of the fundamental need for fairer distributions of wealth and greater social justice are dismissed out of hand as if they have been consigned to the political archives. In any case, any coherent political ideologies in which people, social policy and our social ecology are given priority over economic imperatives do not stand a chance of gaining power nor surviving for long if they did. For any individual government to stand in the way of the flow of the tide of international capital, or to try and swim against it, would lead to a swift crushing.

As well as the inexorable drift of Western politics towards a central free market position, the collapse of communism and the opening up of hitherto inaccessible economies in the Far East are just some of the economic successes of the new global market. In the face of this financial glacier, mountains will move. At one and the same time, however, the global market has unleashed untold economic instability and human misery and, despite its stated intentions, widespread economic chaos. While the Western governments rubbed their hands with glee at the collapse of the former Soviet Union and the former East Euro-

pean communist countries, the alternative free market economies that have been imposed in exchange for loans have led to
economic collapse. Instead of stability and development, what
has been unleashed has been uninhibited corruption, widening
inequalities and increasing levels of violence. The Russian economy is in turmoil and on the brink of collapse with inflation
spiralling out of control. The economies of Indonesia, Malaysia,
the Far East, Latin America and Japan are also all in turmoil.
Even Japan's economy, for so long the envy of the industrialized
world, has been wrecked by the destructive flow of international
capital. Japan's long-term-oriented banking and financial institutions, its system of lifetime employment, and ethic of work
commitment and loyalty have been systematically dismantled.
As I write, unemployment there has reached an all-time high,
approaching American levels for the first time in recorded history. Even those who have made billions on the world financial
markets are now raising serious concerns about the sus-
tainability and viability of the system as it currently operates.
George Soros recently wrote in his *Crisis in Global Capitalism*
that the economic, political and social instability that we have
witnessed over recent years is not a transient fluctuation of the
unregulated flow of capital, but an inevitable consequence of
the way it operates. Soros describes the flow of money around
the world's financial markets as a wrecking ball crashing about
destructively from one economy to another.[47]

The World Bank and the International Monetary Fund (IMF)
were set up after the Second World War to oversee global economic order. The IMF makes short-term loans to countries to
help them deal with economic emergencies, while the World
Bank raises cash on global financial markets and has a longer-
term role in reconstructing war-damaged countries and, supposedly, alleviating poverty and deprivation around the globe. The
truth that these institutions preach is of course the simple laws
of free market economics. They may offer loans to struggling
national economies or concessions on existing interest payments,
but any such financial assistance is highly conditional. In order
to qualify, national governments have to succumb to the higher
truth that is free market economics and to adopt market-friendly

policies. By withholding or withdrawing loans these institutions not only have the financial clout to insist on the implementation of market reforms, but they can also bring about political change. Unsuitable governments that do not convert to the market economies can quite literally be removed. In their marvellous critique of the World Bank's inherent failures and contradictions, Susan George and Fabrizio Sabelli point to another important aspect of the impact of market forces. In order to change societies, people's beliefs about themselves and their relationship to their society, their attitudes and their values must also be altered:

> To change society one must also change individual men and women. Man must be ontologically reconstructed and redeemed as *Homo Economicus*. What is redemption if not the passage from one state to another, from darkness to light? The virtues of the New Economic Man, whose dwelling place is the market, are the will and the capacity to accumulate, to follow self-interest and to maximize profit in all things. His wants are unlimited; to satisfy them, he must learn to struggle against his fellows. Scarcity is a fact of life. There is not enough to satisfy the unlimited desires of all, nor to provide a place in the sun for everyone. If unemployment in their country is 20 per cent or more, the New Men and Women will pit themselves against each other to find work at any price, at all costs.[48]

While we are busy competing against each other for diminishing resources – for employment, for green spaces, for time and money – we cannot afford to stop to consider why it is that those resources are diminishing in the first place. Such considerations are obscure, and the reasons for scarcity in such an otherwise immensely wealthy country are abstract and removed from ordinary life. Instead of focusing outwards and critically examining the ways in which our lives have been restructured, we are encouraged to turn against each other, our children and ourselves. A system based on competition for limited and uncertain resources will inevitably inhibit co-operation and promote aggression. Under such conditions people's behaviour towards their fellows will harden, and their cultural frameworks will shift in ways that reflect this. Thus we are told to believe that scarcity is a fact of life and inequality is the 'natural order'. Economic deprivation among large sections of the population in a country with vast resources is merely an extension of evolutionary principles and the 'survival of the fittest'. In other words, some believe that those at the bottom of the heap are essentially there because they are inherently weak or because they choose to be, and that with a bit more effort they too could partake of the cake of life. Indeed, at a time when the inequalities in society grow ever larger and deprivation and exclusion become more widespread, it cannot be a coincidence that there has been a proliferation of simplistic and highly individualistic explanations for every facet of human experience, suffering and, of course, violent behaviour.

The more centralized power has become, particularly economic power in the hands of fewer organizations run by fewer people, so responsibility has been devolved downwards to the level of the individual. Instead of a morality that emphasizes our collective responsibilities, the individualized concept of 'personal responsibility' has become the defining framework of late twentieth-century Britain. It is seen by many as both an explanation for the obvious decline in moral standards in society and a viable solution: if only more people exercised greater levels of it, then we would all be better off. Yet orthodox free-market principles are devoid of morality, and unfettered free-market practices do not operate with responsibility. The only principle in this deadly game is the imperative to maximize profits and the acquisition of wealth. There are no rules, no regulations, no code of conduct, no ethics and there is no fair play. In a system based on market economics and ruthless competition, there can only be winners and losers. The individuals who bear the worst consequences of this are also frequently the ones who express themselves violently or who become crippled by distress. Offenders are routinely asked to exercise greater awareness of the consequences of their actions for other people. Those who operate on the world's financial markets, however, only have to consider the consequences of their actions in purely economic terms.

Responsibility is a two-way process. Each and every violent crime committed is a sign that the wider community has failed, often appallingly so, in its responsibility to look after that particular citizen. It is pointless people talking about a decline in moral standards and for politicians to posture about 'family values' when the economics of the free market is itself morally void and generates material and social conditions that totally undermine family life. Family values based upon stability, responsibility and commitment require financial institutions and an economy that is based upon long-term investment and social policy and not simply short-term economic returns. The survival of families, notions of community, of citizenship, of belonging and participation all require a social and political system based upon inclusion – not one that marginalizes and exploits large sections of its membership. Responsible citizens require economic and cultural values that act responsibly towards them in return. The individual is defined as both personally responsible and capable of exercising choice, and yet for those who are left out, marginalized and crushed at the bottom of the social heap, choices are severely restricted. It is a very short step from a framework of personal responsibility and choice to a compassionless culture of blame.

Market forces cannot be seen – they are abstract and conceptually removed from people's lives – but their consequences are clearly felt and endured. It is hard for people to understand why their lives have changed or why it is that society has become harsher, less tolerant and more violent. Unable to identify quite how or why this has come about, the only choice we have left is to implode: to blame each other and ourselves. Child abuse and other forms of violence are part of a much bigger picture of widening inequalities, increasing levels of poverty and widespread economic insecurity. The experience of poverty and deprivation, as well as the distorted cultural values this generates, are closely linked to the rising levels of violence in society. Much of that violence takes place within a society that is organized in such a way as to make such experiences an inevitable consequence for many of its citizens. As long as we continue to define violent individuals as evil, to demonize them, or else in some way to medicalize them, then the social, economic and political context in which their violence developed is effectively obscured from view.

At the same time as the individual has become more vulnerable, isolated and at the mercy of unrestricted forces of barely imaginable ferocity, so it is that highly individualistic versions of both medicine and psychology have come to dominate our cultural frameworks. Of course, those frameworks have themselves been shaped by economic pressures and professional self-interest and the need to survive and compete in a market. The certainties with which the scientific community proclaim their findings and offer individual solutions to the degradation of our social ecology serve only to further obscure any meaningful examination of the condition that we now find ourselves in. This occurs both at a cultural level, whereby these professions contribute to the frameworks we operate within, as well as at an individual level – when people turn to these professions for help. Psychiatry in particular is often guilty of the worst forms of ideological distortion by individualizing and defining as deviant those experiences that are in fact widespread and increasingly common. Unfortunately, psychology, psychotherapy and the counselling industry, which are all in a position to shed light upon the ecological nature of the problems they deal with, all too readily collude in this same process of distortion. This is the ultimate form of disempowerment, whereby the reasons for people's suffering, their struggles to cope with the demands placed upon them, the breakdown of their relationships, their abuse of or indifference to their children: these reasons are systematically obscured by a moral and professional rhetoric of individual responsibility and choice, and a scientific rhetoric that finds their bodies deficient and their genes inadequate.

Whenever there is media coverage of a violent crime or the exploitation of a child, it is right that people should be outraged, angry and moved by what they see and hear. However, that outrage and condemnation needs more than ever to be tempered by an awareness of what the perpetrator of the crime will have been through; what such people will have experienced in order

213

to learn to express themselves destructively. Indeed, the more vicious, obscene or hideous their crime, then the more terrible their experience will, in all probability, have been. Any moral condemnation also needs to be softened by the fact that they will have been at the mercy of forces that, as for most of us, they have been utterly powerless to do anything about. If it is said that the perpetrator of the crime came from a happy home in a basically benign world, then don't believe that to be true.

Notes

2 Making Sense: Towards a Social Ecology

1. Box, S. (1983), *Power, Crime and Mystification*, Routledge & Kegan Paul.
2. Our individual ability to think, plan, concentrate and remember develops out of the social processes through which our culture is handed to us as we learn to use language. The process in which our initial social interactions form the basis for our (partially) individualized mental faculties has been brilliantly described by the Russian psychologist Lev Vygotsky in his two major works, *Thought and Language* (1962), Cambridge, MIT, and Wiley (originally published in Russian in 1934); and *Mind in Society: The Development of Higher Psychological Processes* (1978), Harvard University Press.
3. Moir, A. and Jessel, D. (1995), *A Mind to Crime. The Controversial Link between the Mind and Criminal Behaviour*, Signet.
4. Credit to Janet Bostock from whom I have borrowed this metaphor – it's possible she may have borrowed it from someone else!
5. Marshall, J. R. (1986), 'Hereditary Aspects of Schizophrenia: A Critique', in Eiesenberg, N. and Glasgow, D. (eds.), *Current Issues in Clinical Psychology*, Gower.
6. Vaughan, M. (1991), *Curing Their Ills: Colonial Power and African Illness*. Polity Press. Megan Vaughan's detailed and critical analysis of the role of medicine and psychiatry in colonial Africa is as illuminating about colonialism as it is about modern psychiatric practices. It provides a strikingly clear analysis of the relationship between power and knowledge.

215

7. Showalter, E. (1987), 'The Female Malady: Women, Madness and English Culture, 1830–1980', in Vaughan, M. (1991), *Curing Their Ills: Colonial Power and African Illness*, Polity Press.
8. Carothers, J. C. (1953), *The African Mind in Health and Disease*, Geneva, p. 177.
9. Whether an antisocial offender is categorized as having a diagnosis of psychopathy depends not only on which psychiatrist they are interviewed by, but also on such other vagaries as to which prison the offender is remanded to. I have also seen huge differences between men and women in this regard; for example, if a woman has a tattoo this is viewed as indicative of psychopathy, yet in men this is disregarded. There are many studies that have demonstrated the value-laden judgements made in so-called psychiatric diagnoses. For an example of this in psychopathy, see Chiswick, D. (1992), 'The Compulsory Treatment of Patients with a Psychopathic Disorder: An Abnormally Aggressive or Seriously Irresponsible Exercise', *Criminal Behaviour and Mental Health*, 2, 2, pp. 106–13.
10. Countless studies have failed to identify a single type of 'abnormal' personality that behaves in antisocial ways. As such, the term 'psychopathy' is so vague as to encompass any form of antisocial behaviour. See Blackburn, R. (1988), 'On Moral Judgements and Personality Disorders: The Myth of Psychopathic Disorder Revisited', *British Journal of Psychiatry*, 153, pp. 505–12.
11. While there is a widely held belief in the medical validity of the term 'psychopath' (psychopathic personality), there is in fact no such diagnostic category. Psychopathic disorder is a legal term defined under the Mental Health Act 1983 as 'a persistent disorder or disability of mind (whether or not including significant impairment of intelligence) which results in abnormally aggressive or seriously irresponsible conduct on the part of the person concerned' (The Mental Health Act 1983, p. 2). Under the equivalent legislation in Scotland, the category of psychopathy does not exist. It is therefore not seen as a treatable condition in Scotland, and so any offenders put into this category are sent to prison and not to forensic or psychiatric secure hospitals.
12. The late Richard Marshall critically analysed all of the available 'evidence' for a genetic basis to schizophrenia and discovered several methodological flaws, conceptual errors and blind leaps of ideological faith. For a review of his work see, for example, Marshall, J. R. (1996), 'Science, Schizophrenia and Genetics: The Creation of Myths', *Journal of Primary Prevention*, 17, no. 1.

13. James, O. (1995), *Juvenile Violence in a Winner–Loser Culture: Socio-economic and Familial Origins of the Rise of Violence against the Person*, Free Association Books. In fact, at the time James wrote his book the increase was thirty-fold.
14. Carey, G. (1989), 'Genetics and Violence: Human Studies', in James, *Juvenile Violence*, p. 94.
15. James, *Juvenile Violence*, p. 93.

3 The Past and Future: The Legacy of Child Abuse

1. In the technical jargon of psychiatry, when distress is experienced as a more or less persistent feature of a person's life it is said to be 'chronic' as opposed to 'acute', and 'endogenous' as opposed to 'reactive'. That is, the distress does not seem to be a response to recent on-going life events, but persists regardless of the current circumstances the person finds themselves in.

2. In the early part of his theorizing, Freud discovered that many of his clients had been sexually abused when they were children by adult male relatives and that this accounted for their subsequent problems as adults that he saw in terms of their 'hysteria'. He was, however, faced with intense resistance to this notion from the powerful and wealthy circles in Vienna where he lived, and which provided him with his clients and also his professional credibility. Bowing to these vested interests, he did as profound a theoretical 'U' turn as is possible by transforming the genuine disclosures of sexual abuse that he heard from his clients into the wishful and fantasy-based desires of their childhood imaginations. In other words, he distorted and concealed the sexual abuse of innocent children by turning those children into active sexual participants in a previously undiscovered subconscious world. For a particularly detailed account of this process, see Jeffrey Masson (1990), *The Assault on Truth: Freud's Suppression of the Seduction Theory*, Fontana.

3. The detailed study of children's adaptations for coping with different forms of abuse has been carried out over decades by Patricia Crittenden of the University of Miami. Her largely observational work is particularly revealing for those who are interested in the strategies and interactional styles that children adopt when they are being maltreated. Until recently, the main attempts to link distress in adults to trauma and abuses in childhood have mainly come from psychotherapists working with adults. Many of these

theories have been based on the adult's accounts of being abused (which is informative in itself), yet many psychotherapeutic theories have attempted to explain the effects of abuse in terms of the intra-psychic activity of the children, to which of course they have no privileged access. As such, they have spent a lot of energy pondering what was going on inside a child when they would do far better to watch what children are showing them through their behaviour and the way in which they relate to others once they have been abused. Crittenden's lifetime work has at times involved observing maltreated children into adulthood, and watching them as they become parents themselves. Examples of her extensive work include: Crittenden, P. M. (1992), 'Children's Strategies for Coping with Adverse Home Environments: An Interpretation Using Attachment Theory', *Child Abuse and Neglect*, 16, pp. 329–33; Crittenden, P. M. (1995), 'Attachment and Risk for Psychopathology: The Early Years', *Developmental and Behavioural Paediatrics*, 16, 3, pp. 12–16; Crittenden, P. M. and DiLalla, D. L. (1988), 'Compulsive Compliance: The Development of an Inhibitory Coping Strategy in Infancy', *Journal of Abnormal Child Psychology*, 16, 5, pp. 585–99.

4. For a thorough review of this literature, see Oliver James (1995), *Juvenile Violence in a Winner–Loser Culture: Socio-economic and Familial Origins of the Rise of Violence against the Person*, Free Association Books, chapter 1.

5. Laing, R. D. and Esterson, A. (1964), *Sanity, Madness and the Family*, Tavistock Publications.

6. Vaughn, G. E., Snyder, K. S., Freeman, W., Jones, S., Falloon, I. R. H., and Lieberman, R. P. (1982), 'Family Factors in Schizophrenic Relapse: A Replication', *Schizophrenic Bulletin*, 8, pp. 425–6; Vaughn, G. E. and Leff, J. P. (1976), 'The Influence of Family and Social Factors on the Course of Psychiatric Illness', *British Journal of Psychiatry*, 129, pp. 125–37.

7. Goldstein, M. J. and Douane, J. A. (1982), 'Family Factors in the Onset, Course and Treatment of Schizophrenic Spectrum Disorders', *Journal of Nervous and Mental Diseases*, 170, pp. 692–700: It is difficult to: 'view family life as so discontinuous across life-span that those attributes of the family environment related to the onset of schizophrenia do not overlap with those associated with differential course after an initial episode' (p. 693).

8. For a detailed account of powerlessness as well as the other principal consequences of childhood sexual abuse (betrayal, stigmatization, traumatic sexualization), see Finkelhor, D. (1986), *A Source*

Book in Child Abuse, Sage; or Finkelhor, D. (1987), 'The Trauma of Child Sexual Abuse – Two Models', *Journal of Interpersonal Violence*, 12, 4, pp. 348–66.

9. Smail, D. (1993), *The Origins of Unhappiness: A New Understanding of Personal Distress*, HarperCollins.

10. There are several studies that have systematically linked the experience of childhood violence to the presentation of distress in adult women patients in psychiatric hospitals as well as community settings. These have found that between 50 and 80 per cent of women using psychiatric services have histories of childhood sexual or physical abuse, or that they had witnessed domestic violence. These studies include women who are diagnosed as untreatable 'psychotic' and 'borderline personality disordered' – long-term patients as well as those who have used acute services. Among these studies are: Beck, J. C. and Van der Kolk, B. A. (1987), 'Reports of Childhood Incest and Current Behaviour of Chronically Hospitalised Psychotic Women', *American Journal of Psychiatry*, 144, 11, pp. 1474–6; Bryer, J. B., Nelson, B. A., Miller, J. B., and Krol, P. A. (1987), 'Childhood Sexual Abuse and Physical Abuse as Factors in Adult Psychiatric Illness', *American Journal of Psychiatry*, 144, 11, pp. 1426–31; Herman, J. L., Perry, J. C., and Van der Kolk, B. A. (1989), 'Childhood Trauma in Borderline Personality Disorder', *American Journal of Psychiatry*, 146, 4, pp. 490–5; Rose, S. M., Peabody, C. G., and Stratigeas, B. (1991), 'Undetected Abuse among Intensive Case Management Clients', *Hospital and Community Psychiatry*, 42, 5, pp. 499–503; Walker, S. and James, H. (1992), 'Childhood Physical and Sexual Abuse in Women', *Psychiatry in Practice*, 11, 1, pp. 15–18.

11. *Diagnostic and Statistical Manual of Mental Disorders* (4th edition) (1997), American Psychiatric Association, Washington DC.

12. *ICD-10 Classification of Mental and Behavioural Disorders* (1992), World Health Organization, Geneva.

4 Victims and Perpetrators

1. Gitta Sereny (1995), *The Case of Mary Bell*, Pimlico.
2. Gitta Sereny (1998), *Cries Unheard*, Macmillan.
3. Smith, D. J. (1994), *The Sleep of Reason: The James Bulger Case*, Century, p. 188.
4. Smith, *The Sleep of Reason*, p. 7.
5. *Guardian*, 25 November 1993.

6. *Guardian*, 25 November 1993.
7. Newson, E. (1994), 'Video Violence and the Protection of Children', *ACPP Review and Newsletter*, 16, 4, pp. 190–5.
8. Thomas, M. (1993), *Every Mother's Nightmare: The Killing of James Bulger*, Pan, p. 266.
9. Smith, *The Sleep of Reason*, p. 188.
10. *Children of Crime*, Tuesday, 7 April 1998, BBC1.
11. Smith, *The Sleep of Reason*, p. 139.
12. Gitta Sereny, 'Approaching the Truth', *Independent on Sunday*, 13 February 1994.
13. Smith, *The Sleep of Reason*, p. 153.
14. Sereny, *The Case of Mary Bell*, p. 329.
15. Sereny, *The Case of Mary Bell*, p. 325.
16. Nicci Gerrard, *Observer*, 26 November 1995.
17. *The Times*, 23 November 1995.
18. *The Times*, 23 November 1995.
19. *Guardian*, 23 November 1995.
20. *Guardian*, 23 November 1995.
21. *Guardian*, 23 November 1995.
22. *Guardian*, 23 November 1995.

5 Troubled Children, Troubled Adults

1. The Children's Society (1998), *No Lessons Learnt*.
2. *People Like Us* (1997), HMSO.
3. *Independent*, 20 November 1997.
4. *Guardian*, 20 November 1997.
5. *Guardian*, 20 November 1997.
6. *Violent Victims* (1995), Prince's Trust.
7. *Guardian*, 13 May 1998.
8. *Independent*, 20 November 1997.
9. Social Services Inspectorate.
10. Given their horrific backgrounds, it seems incongruous that the predominant forms of psychological therapy that patients are offered are essentially rationalistic or cognitive approaches which continue to be the vogue at present throughout the world of psychological treatments. Even where it is acknowledged that psychological factors or violent behaviour are traceable to early traumatic experiences such as physical or sexual abuse or chaotic relationships, most forms of psychological therapies are typically divorced from these insights. Instead of dealing directly with the

impact of these experiences, the target for intervention becomes decontextualized psychological or behavioural processes.

11. The extent to which a person's background and experience of victimization can be taken into account as a legal defence for their own act of violence is virtually non-existent. In order to avoid a conviction for murder, which carries with it a mandatory life sentence, one has to prove a breakdown of the assumed rationality which so much of the legal and psychiatric system is based on, i.e. the notion of diminished responsibility. Diminished responsibility is a virtually meaningless concept from a psychological point of view. The most obvious grounds for defence on the grounds of diminished responsibility is to medicalize the perpetrator by defining them as mentally disordered and, as I have indicated, there are huge problems with this as a meaningful explanation. Defining someone as disordered is the only way in which the effects of child abuse can be *indirectly* taken into account as defence. Alternatively, the perpetrator may have acted on the grounds of provocation. The law on provocation, which until very recently had been set by Mr Justice Devlin in 1949, had to involve a 'sudden and temporary loss of control' in the heat of the moment, 'without a sufficient time gap before reason is restored'. In 1992 Kiranjit Ahluwahlia was freed by an Appeal Court in a ground-breaking ruling that changed her original conviction for murder to that of manslaughter. She had poured petrol and set fire to her brutal husband as he lay sleeping at home. The judges in her appeal removed the need to show the defendant acted immediately to provocation, i.e. not sudden and immediate anger, but anger that has boiled-up over a period – she still acted in 'hot blood', but not in haste. In the Ahluwahlia appeal, the judges began to accept for the first time that the long-term cumulative effects of domestic violence can be taken into account as provocation. Until that point, if there was no diminished responsibility on the grounds of provocation, then the only alternative must be a conviction for murder. This extended definition certainly does not extend to provocation over the distant time-span and different relationships that would be involved with the experience of child abuse, particularly if the victim of the subsequent crime was someone other than the original perpetrator of the abuse.

12. For a review of the characteristics of psychiatric hospitals and those for patients with disabilities that have been subject to public inquiries up until the mid-1980s, see Martin, J. P. (1984), *Hospitals in Trouble*, Basil-Blackwell.

13. Boynton, J. (Chair), *Report on the Review of Rampton Hospital* (DHSS) (1980), HMSO.
14. Blom-Cooper, L. (Chair) (1992), *Report of the Committee of Inquiry into Complaints about Ashworth Hospital*, vols 1 and 2, CM 2029/1, HMSO.
15. *Guardian*, 6 August 1992.
16. *Independent*, 6 August 1992.
17. Blom-Cooper, *Report of the Committee of Inquiry*, p. 146.
18. Blom-Cooper, *Report of the Committee of Inquiry*, p. 229.
19. Potier, M. A. (1993), 'Giving Evidence: Women's Lives in Ashworth Maximum Security Psychiatric Hospital', *Feminism and Psychology*, 3, 3, pp. 335–47 (p. 345).
20. Gitta Sereny (1995), *The Case of Mary Bell*, Pimlico, p. xi.
21. Gitta Sereny (1998), *Cries Unheard*, Macmillan.
22. In other countries the concept of dangerousness can be applied to all sexual offenders and not just those defined as mentally disordered, as is the case in Britain. In California, for example, there is a legal concept of a 'mentally disordered sex offender' which does allow for the assessment of future conduct based upon an individual's probability of reoffending. The present Labour government is considering a Crime and Disorder Bill which, if it becomes law, will permit a mandatory life sentence for a second serious sexual offence, thus putting the punishment on par with murder.
23. *Criminal Statistics England and Wales*, 1994, 1997. An annual publication of the Government Statistical Service, HMSO. See 'Offences currently recorded as homicide where the victim was aged under 16 and a suspect had been identified who was not known to the victim'.
24. *Criminal Statistics England and Wales*, 1994, 1997. See 'Violence against the person by sex of victim and location'.
25. *Criminal Statistics England and Wales*, 1994, 1997. See 'Offences currently recorded as homicide by relationship of victim to principal suspect'.

6 Violence in Society

1. *British Crime Survey*, 1994, 1996, 1997, Home Office.
2. *Criminal Statistics England and Wales*. An annual publication of the Government Statistical Service, HMSO. Each year of publication refers to the data gathered for that particular calendar year.

NOTES

3. *Criminal Statistics England and Wales*, 1996, 1997. 'Violent Offences', in this context only refers to the combined totals of 'Violence against the Person' and 'Sexual Offences', and excludes the Home Office definition of 'Violent Offences', which includes burglaries and theft, etc.

Total of all notifiable offences in 1997 was 4,595,200. The total for all 'Sexual Offences' that year was 33,500 (0.73 percent of the total).

Total of all 'Violent Offences' ('Violence against the Person' and 'Sexual Offences') in 1997 was 286,000. 'Sexual Offences' therefore represent 11.7 percent of this figure.

Total of all notifiable offences in 1996 was 5,036,600. Total for all 'Sexual Offences' that year was 31,400 (0.63 percent).

Total of all 'Violent Offences' ('Violence against the Person' and 'Sexual Offences') in 1996 was 270,700. 'Sexual Offences' therefore represent 11.6 percent of this figure.

These percentages are consistent for all of the years from 1984 onwards.

4. *Criminal Statistics England and Wales*, 1994.

Total number of offenders found guilty of 'Sexual Offences' 1984–94 = 63,900.
Total number of females convicted of 'Sexual Offences' is less than 1,000 (1.5 percent of total).

Total number of offenders found guilty of 'Violence against the Person' offences 1984–94 = 472,000.
Total number of females convicted in all courts for 'Violence against the Person' offences is 41,600 (8.8 percent of total).

Total number of offenders found guilty for all indictable offences 1984–94 = 4,016,900.
Total number of females convicted for all indictable offences is 508,700 (11.3 percent of total).

5. *British Crime Survey*, 1998, Home Office.
6. *Criminal Statistics England and Wales*, 1970, 1994, 1996, 1997. Figures are rounded off to the nearest 1,000.
7. *Criminal Statistics England and Wales*, 1970, 1994, 1996 and

1997. In 1950 the incidence of crimes of 'Violence against the Person' was a total of just 6,000; by 1959 this had doubled to 12,000, and by 1969 it had reached 27,000. The 1970s saw significant rises so that by the end of that decade the figure had reached 95,000. In 1986 the figure was 125,000, and in 1997 it had risen to 253,000. Therefore the increase from 1950 to the end of 1986 was 119,000. The increase from the beginning of 1987 to the end of 1997 was 128,000.

8. Overall reported crime dropped by 1 percent in 1993, 5 percent in 1994, 3 percent in 1995, 1 percent in 1996, and 9 percent in 1997 – taking the total below 5 million for the first time since 1989. In complete contrast to these reductions, the figures for 'Violence against the Person' and 'Sexual Offences' have increased every year over this period of time. For example, in 1994, while overall crime dropped by 5 percent, 'Violence against the Person' rose by 7 percent and 'Sexual Offences' by 2 percent.

   In 1997, while overall recorded crime fell by 9 percent, 'Violence against the Person' rose by 6 percent (an increase of 13,800 to 253,100) and 'Sexual Offences' up 7 percent (an increase of 2,100 to 33,500). Rapes rose by 12 percent to 6,337, a figure that includes 342 rapes of men, which was not previously a recordable crime. Contrast these increases with decreases in overall crimes against property (which make up 90 per cent of recorded crime), which fell by 10 per cent. Robbery and burglary both dropped by 14 percent and 13 percent respectively; criminal damage and theft, and handling stolen goods both dropped by 9 percent.

9. *British Crime Survey*, 1998. The most recent *British Crime Survey* indicates a drop in overall violent crime for the first time. Though violent crime has doubled overall in the last decade, the survey shows it peaked in 1994, consistently rising from 1981 and then down, for the most recent years, between 1995 and 1997.

10. James, O. (1995), *Juvenile Violence in a Winner–Loser Culture: Socio-economic and Familiar Origins of the Rise of Violence against the Person*, Free Association Books. In a review of the figures for the period 1987–93, James found that the rate per 100,000 of recorded juvenile (ten- to sixteen-year-olds) 'Violence against the Person' rose by 40.5 percent, in stark contrast to the fact that over the same period the total for all juvenile offences decreased by 26 percent. Similarly, the number of recorded violent juveniles increased by 34 percent while at the same time the number cautioned or found guilty of *all* crimes *decreased* by 31 percent. Compared to the figures for previous years this has

been an increase on a scale that has not been seen before: between 1980 and 1987 the rate of juvenile violent offending rose by only 2 percent and the numbers of offenders actually fell by 15.5 percent.

Comparison of these figures for juvenile violence with other crimes show the extent of the increase in violence: over the same period recorded offences for juveniles for theft and handling stolen goods actually fell by 40 per cent – virtually the same amount as for violence, but in the opposite direction. The actual number of offenders for the theft group *fell* by 42.5 percent as opposed to the 34 percent *increase* for violence.

11. James (1995), *Juvenile Violence*. 'Violence against the Person' offences made up 4 percent of all crimes committed by ten- to thirteen-year-olds in 1987. By 1993 this was 9 percent. For four-teen- to sixteen-year-olds, the rise was from 8 percent to 13 percent over the same period of time.

12. The number of fourteen- to twenty-year-old males, the most visibly violent group, has fallen in numbers by a fifth since 1987.

13. Hutton, W. (1995), *The State We're In*, Vintage, p. 168.

14. Summarizing his review of the literature on physically and verbally abusive families, in *Juvenile Violence*, James wrote: 'There are no developed nations in which high-income families are more abusive than the low-income families ... Taken as a whole, the evidence leaves little room for doubt that [physical] abuse and the severe punishment that accompanies it are significantly more likely in families with low-incomes, manual professional occupations and low educational attainment' (p. 48). See also Gelles, R. J. and Cornell, C. P. (1985), *Intimate Violence in Families*, Sage.

15. Hutton, *The State We're In*, p. 92.

16. Joseph Rowntree Foundation (1995), *Income and Wealth: Report of the Joseph Rowntree Foundation Inquiry Group*, York. The real income of the poorest 10 per cent of the British population fell by 17 percent during the period 1979–92 compared with a 62 percent rise in real income for the wealthiest 10 per cent. See also Jenkins, S. (1994), *Winners and Losers, A Portrait of the UK Income Distribution in the 1980s*, Joseph Rowntree Findings Series.

17. *Households Below Average Income* (1997). A statistical analysis for 1979–1994–5. This is a publication of the Government Statistical Office, HMSO. These figures cover the period up to and including the end of the 1995 financial year, i.e. up to spring 1996.

18. *Human Development Report* (1998), the United Nations Develop-

ment Programme, Oxford University Press. The personal fortune
of Bill Gates, the richest man in the world as well as the richest
American, has now topped £40 billion – more than the combined
wealth of the poorest 100 million Americans.

19. Currie, E. (1985), *Confronting Crime*, Pantheon, New York,
p. 171.
20. I have personally worked with many adults who have had fathers,
husbands and grandfathers who were brutal, violent and destructive for many years after they returned from both of the world
wars. I have also had experience of working with a small number
of very traumatized Falklands and Gulf War veterans, who have
also shown tendencies towards violence on their return home.
Given that these latter conflicts were much smaller in scale in terms
of the proportion of the male population involved, their impact
on the levels of violence in the wider society has also been more
limited. Many of the veterans I have seen have been unable to
hang on to or maintain personal relationships, and some have been
subsequently convicted and imprisoned because of their violent
conduct.

It is not just the direct experience of combat and of carnage
that has been the most damaging aspect of conflict for these men.
For example, the impact of being a long-term prisoner of war is
known to have mental health implications for those involved many
decades after the events. Just as in child abuse and other forms of
prolonged violence, long-term war imprisonment involves a
chronic state of powerlessness, uncertainty and threat. As the end
of the Second World War drew nearer, these conditions of uncertainty and threat worsened as many prisoners feared that they
would be killed prior to their particular camp being liberated. See,
for example, Sutker, P. B., Allain, A. N., and Winstead, D. K.
(1993), 'Psychopathology and Psychiatric Diagnoses of World War
Two Pacific Theatre Prisoner of War Survivors and Combat Veterans', *American Journal of Psychiatry*, 150, 2, pp. 240–5; and
Engdahl, B. E., Speed, N., Eberly, R. E., and Schwartz, J. (1991),
'Co-morbidity of Psychiatric Disorders and Personality Profiles of
American World War Two Prisoners of War', *Journal of Nervous
and Mental Disease*, 179, pp. 181–7.
21. Krohn, M. (1976), 'Inequality, Unemployment and Crime: A
Cross-national Analysis', *Sociological Quarterly*, 17.
22. Currie, *Confronting Crime*, p. 173.
23. Hutton, *The State We're In*, p. 106. Beyond those (1.7 million in
1995) who are claiming unemployment benefit, there are another

2 million who do not qualify as they cannot prove they are actively seeking work or because there is none for them to do. About half of these are classified as long-term sick and thus eligible for sickness and invalidity benefit. According to the *Households Below Average Income* figures, a quarter of those in the bottom fifth income bracket live in families described as 'other' – the long-term sick, the disabled and non-working single parents, a figure that has more than doubled since 1979 (2.7 million to 5.8 million people).

24. *Households Below Average Income.*
25. *British Crime Survey*, 1998.
26. Smith, L. J. F. (1989), *Domestic Violence: An Overview of the Literature*, a Home Office research and planning report, HMSO.
27. Townsend, P. and Davidson, N. (1982), *Inequalities in Health Care: The Black Report*, Penguin. There has been consistent evidence linking social inequality and poverty to ill health and lower life expectancy, but this report was a seminal study in this respect.
28. Bruce, M. L., Takeuchi, D. T., and Leaf, P. J. (1991), 'Poverty and Psychiatric Status: Longitudinal Evidence from the New Haven Epidemiological Catchment Area Study', *Archives of General Psychiatry*, 48, 5, pp. 470–4. The direct links between poverty and distress have been consistently well documented, particularly the correlation between low income and depression.
29. *Social Trends*, 26 (1996), HMSO.
30. Wilkinson, R. (1994), *Unfair Shares*, Barnardos.
31. *Households Below Average Income.*
32. Hutton, *The State We're In*. In 1995 there were more than 5 million people working part time, 80 per cent of whom were women. Some 2 million work for sixteen hours or less a week with virtually no protection or employment rights. More than three-quarters of part-time jobs are defined as low-paid – earning two-thirds or less than the average wage. Two-thirds of all new jobs offered to the unemployed are part-time or temporary.
33. *Households Below Average Income.*
34. National Society for the Protection of Children (NSPCC (1996), *Children at Risk.*
35. Gelles and Cornell (1985), *Intimate Violence in Families.*
36. OECD (Organization for Economic Co-operation and Development) (1994), *Employment Outlook.*
37. Hutton, *The State We're In*, p. 197.
38. The Nuffield Trust (1998). The cost of sickness absence from the NHS is currently about £700 million a year, at a rate of around 5 percent as opposed to in industry where the average is some

3.7 percent. Rates of psychological disturbance, ranging from anxiety to chronic depression, were found to vary from 21 percent to 50 per cent among doctors, and from 29 percent to 48 percent among nurses, and from 33 percent to 50 per cent among managers. This report prompted Sandy Macara, the chairman of the British Medical Association, to state that, 'these findings show that working for the NHS can seriously damage your health' (reported in the *Guardian*, 25 March 1998).

39. *Households Below Average Income.* In 1979 7 percent of families were headed by lone parents; in 1996 this had risen to 18 percent. The proportion of the poorest section of society that are lone parents has increased dramatically. In 1979 single parents made up only 9 percent of the bottom quintile compared to almost a quarter (23 percent) of that income group by 1996. One-parent families are concentrated at the bottom end of the income range, with over half of the total population of single parents (overwhelmingly women) within the bottom 20 per cent.

40. The Children's Society (1998), *No Lessons Learnt.* In the 1996–7 academic year alone, there were 137,000 temporary expulsions and a record 2.2 million school days were lost by children temporarily or permanently excluded.

41. As we have seen, in order to make sense of the detrimental effects on children of modern patterns of social organization, we have inevitably turned to medical explanations and to the pathologization of children rather than focusing firmly on the malign and often chaotic conditions under which they have been raised. Thus it seems as if the medical profession has had to invent new diagnostic categories (or broaden the definition of existing ones) with which to view children's adaptations to this chaos and widespread instability. Previously, difficult-to-manage children (usually boys) were seen as being 'hyperactive', but increasingly the categories of Asperger's syndrome and ADHD (Attention-Deficit/Hyperactivity Disorder) are now being applied. Predictably, a chemical solution in the form of the drug Retalin is now the treatment of choice.

42. World Health Report (1995), *Bridging the Gaps*, World Health Organization. The life expectancy of a Ugandan man is in the low forties, while a Japanese woman can expect to live to her late seventies.

43. World Health Report (1995), *Bridging the Gaps.*

44. *Human Development Report* (1998). The gap between richer and poorer countries continues to expand. Of all the money spent on personal consumption, 86 percent is spent by just 20 per cent of

the world's population. At the same time, the poorest 20 per cent account for a mere 1.3 percent of personal consumption.

The report reveals that while Americans spend more than £5 billion a year on cosmetics, and Europeans spend £7 billion on ice cream, it would take only £9 billion to provide universal basic education in all of the world's poorest countries, and about £27 billion would meet all basic needs. In 1997 all of the poorest countries collectively received $25.1 billion in aid, yet the annual world trade in weapons is valued at $22 billion per year and world military spending is $800 billion a year. Britain alone spends $35 billion a year on the military and the USA spends $280 billion a year.

45. George, S. (1990), *Ill Fares the Land. Essays on Food, Hunger and Power*, Penguin.
46. It was economic imperatives that mobilized the Western world to rescue strategically placed oil-laden Kuwait in the Gulf War, while just a few years later, a million Rwandans were left by the international community to be slaughtered in just 100 days.
47. Soros, G. (1998), *Crisis of Global Capitalism*, Little, Brown.
48. George, S. and Sabelli, F. (1994), *Faith and Credit. The World Bank's Secular Empire*, Penguin, pp. 249–50.

Index

Victim Support, 25
victim to perpetrator, 100–5
violence, 12–14, 38
  against the Person, 176–81
  criminal, 42–3
  domestic, 35, 42, 175, 178
  due to childhood trauma,
    71
  due to powerlessness, 71
  effect of, 69, 101–5, 110
  homicide, 177–8, 186, 188
  in war, 40–1
  males and, 51, 60, 99–100,
    104, 107, 177, 197
  poverty and, 186, 188,
    192–3, 196
  supposed genetic tendency
    to, 59, 142
  victim's self-blame, 78,
    97–100, 176
Violent Victims, 154

Walsh, Brian QC, 117
war, attitude to violence in,
  40–1, 189
West, Anne-Marie, 24, 125,
  129, 131, 132
West, Charmaine, 23–4,
  129–30
West, Fred, 22–5, 40, 97,
  124–33, 156
West, Heather, 22–3, 24, 125,
  129
West, Rose, 22–5, 40, 97,
  124–33, 156
Wilkinson, Richard, 195
witches, 58, 60
Woodward, Louise, 39
work, changing face of,
  199–206
World Bank, 208, 209, 210
World Health Organization,
  206–7